A DEFENSE OF FREEMASONRY

First Edition 1874
A.F.A. Woodford, M.A.

New Edition 2021
Edited by Tarl Warwick

A DEFENSE OF FREEMASONRY

COPYRIGHT AND DISCLAIMER

FOREWORD

This book is a categorical defense of Freemasonry from some contemporary claims against it, written by an actual member of the order. Some of the claims against Masons are still peddled to this day, mostly by extremely "religious" groups which have interpreted symbology and pantomime as literal, or which do not understand basic linguistics (for instance misconstruing the Roman term "Lucifer" as related to the Devil, instead of deriving it from the initial Greek "Phosphoros" which in the Bible is used to describe Jesus, but never Satan.)

Of especial note in this is the specific fixation with the constant persecution of the Catholics against Freemasonry, based largely on spurious claims which could never really be evinced. Since this work comes from the British Empire, it talks at great length about the condemnation of the order for "unlawful oaths"- something civic in nature (generally) with little modern relevance since the age of monarchism has largely ended in much of the Western world.

Sometimes this work waxes slightly theatrical regarding the charity work and spiritual purification the author perceives in his own quasi-occult spiritual path.

This edition of "A Defense of Freemasonry" has been carefully edited for format and content. Care has been taken to retain all original intent and meaning.

A DEFENSE OF FREEMASONRY

DEDICATION

Dear Brother Kenning;

I had great pleasure in asking you to accept the Dedication of this little pamphlet, and still greater on obtaining your kind acceptance of my request.

I dedicate, therefore, this little defense of our common Order to you, because it seems to be the outcome of many fraternal conversations in which your views and mine appeared greatly to harmonize, and because also I am glad in so dedicating this little labor of love to yourself, to record my own deep and grateful appreciation of your laudable desire to encourage in every way the diffusion of a sound Masonic literature in our Craft.

In placing your name then at the head of this dedicatory page, I do it with much personal regard, subscribing myself

Yours always most fraternally,

A. F. A. WOODFORD.

10, Upper Porchester Street,
Hyde Park Square,
London, W.

St. John's Day, 1874.

A DEFENSE OF FREEMASONRY

PREFACE

It has seemed to the writer of this pamphlet that the time had fairly arrived when a few humble words might fitly be said in defense of our good old Craft. For at this moment, though without any apparent reason for it, attacks upon its teaching, its constitution, and its practice seem to abound on every side of us, and to proceed from different schools of thought, and from the most antagonistic bodies of men.

At home and abroad, in Germany and the United States, in Belgium and Brazil, in France and Italy, in Spain and Portugal, the assailants of Freemasonry are many and virulent, and the language alike of diatribe and depreciation, of incrimination and condemnation, is marked by greater bitterness of tone and temper than at any period since 1717.

And yet the banner under which this host of adversaries to Freemasonry is fighting today, is a very motley one indeed!

It seems a little absurd, and it would be very amusing were it not so painful a matter, to find, for instance, Roman Catholics, Reformed Presbyterians, Ritualistic Anglicans, and American Baptists all "rowing in the same boat." And still, nevertheless, so it is.

The Masonic bystander is no doubt anxious to ascertain how this controversial crew will get on, whether like the happy family they will proceed in harmony and dignity, or whether (which is far more likely) they will soon run aground on a mud bank, and "come to grief," and go to pieces!

But be this as it may, in the meantime the attacks on Freemasonry proceed, each succeeding the other in violence of vituperation and acrimony of language, and though I do not say or see that they do Freemasonry or Freemasons much harm in any way, yet it almost appears as if some answer were needed amid this din of controversy, which may encourage our friends and confute our opponents. For the allegations which are made today are precisely the same as those made over and over again before by illogical adversaries, and which, though fully answered, are revived in all the greenness of a fresh growth, and nourish still in the land of the living. One old adversary of Freemasonry is as usual to the fore, the Roman Catholic Church.

"Semper cadem" is still her motto in respect of her hatred and intolerance as regards Freemasonry. Latterly, too, the jubilant tone of the Roman Catholic press, and also of the Ritualistic press, at our late Grand Master's melancholy secession, and at what they both so poetically term the "De profundis" of Freemasonry, has caused that astute religious body, the Roman Catholic Church, to throw off the mask, and to express itself openly in verbiage and views which must startle as they impress every thoughtful mind.

It is quite clear that it is only the want of power which prevents as of old the persecutions and iniquities of the Inquisition.

Rome is still unchanged, and above all things in her hatred to Freemasonry, to light, culture, self-education and toleration. So, rightly or wrongly, I have determined "favente" Bro. Kenning to issue a concise but comprehensive resume of the principal attacks on our order, accompanying it I trust with a not altogether unsuccessful reply.

If my defense of Freemasonry shall meet with the countenance and approval of my brethren, I shall be amply rewarded, as after a membership of thirty-two years, I am glad to be able to avow myself as clearly persuaded as ever, even, perhaps, I may say, more than ever, of the intrinsic excellency, and value, and importance, and need of our fraternity in the present condition of society, and of the world. I am also desirous in this pamphlet of protesting, once for all, against that prevalent unfairness of our opponents of basing their unjustifiable condemnation of our peaceable Order, of our tolerant confraternity, of our philanthropic organization, on the "ex parte" statements of the ignorant, on the ridiculous parodies of the apostate, on the accumulated rubbish of unreasoning accusers, and on the mendacious calumnies of a bye-gone age, hashed up anew today, "usque ad nauseam," by the impugner, the skeptic, the malevolent, and the Jesuit.

So, in all of fraternal sincerity and sympathy, in all of loyalty and elevation to our famous order, I say like the old writer, with some needful little adaptation,

> Go forth, little book, and truly thou me commend
> Unto all "Masons" that desire to learn or understand,
> And specially to them that have experience, praying them
> to amend
> And correct what is amiss, either as a fault or offense,
> And if that any faults be found as prove my negligence,
> Cast the same on my "efforts," rude and bare of
> eloquence,
> Which to draw out I have done my best diligence,
> And readily to reform "them" by reason and better
> sentence.

John Russel's *Book of Nature*, 1460.

A. F. A. W.
St. John's Day, 1874.

A DEFENSE OF FREEMASONRY

A DEFENCE OF FREEMASONRY

The age in which our lot is cast today is marked by many remarkable characteristics. It is an age of great mental activity, careful scientific research, earnest archaeological study, and of much criticism, stern and unsparing enough, no doubt, but not necessarily therefore, permanently unjust, or entirely destructive.

If it be true that each age as it passes on, displays its own character, and that that character is often both special and distinct, we are warranted in saying this much, that the present epoch is happily distinguished by many tokens of intellectual and philanthropic aim, by many elevating and ennobling aspirations, and above all by a general, a fair, a sympathetic spirit. Men have outlived to a great extent, the theories of intolerance and the practices of persecution, and the general tendency of the human mind today, and the wonted scope of the laws of nations are alike inimical to arbitrary or unjust interference with individual liberty of thought, or general professions of belief. But alas! despite this humanizing tone of the present period, the idiosyncracy of our race remains still unchanged, the earnest desire ever existing to impose on others fetters for conscience, or for free thought, too often the only result of all the years of progressive experience and expanding freedom.

It is a most curious chapter in the history of mankind, and in the psychology of the human mind, the apparently innate longing to impress our own convictions on other people, either by state interference or religious pressure.

Looking at the world as it is, there seems to be plenty of margin, humanly speaking, for the antagonistic views and conflicting creeds of churches and of combatants, without attempting to circumscribe our neighbors' freedom of thought and privilege of action. And yet, strangely, if sadly enough, the spirit of Dominic survives the fleeting centuries of time, and reappears in successive eyelets, if perhaps in a new form, and under specious disguises, yet practically still the same animus, unaltered and unaffected, whether it be manifested today by a church, or a state, by a community or by individuals. Indeed, the eagerness to persecute one another for difference of opinion, or divergence of creed, is a very startling fact in itself and a most difficult one to explain satisfactorily, either in the annals or struggles of man.

But so it is, and even in this nineteenth century of ours, we may still hear of, and read numbers of edicts and manifestos; we may still have to listen to public teaching "ex cathedra," and to private opinions and statements which, if carried out to their logical conclusion, would simply encourage and reinforce the revival among us of the days of deliberate persecution, in the too often ill-used name of religion and of truth. Awful parody, painful commentary, on the words and acts of that only Divine teacher who came into this world of ours, speaking to all men words of peace and love; offering to all men a blessed message of healing and reconciliation; at whose gentle bidding the sword was to be sheathed, and angry passions, like elemental strife, were to be stilled; at whose benign intervention, all that separates man from his fellow-man here, or renders man harsh, uncharitable, and intolerant to his fellow-creatures, was to be abolished and obliterated, and pass utterly away.

And though, as I observed at the outset, our own age is characterized by much of very active and kindly sympathy each for each, amid severed and contacted positions in society and the world, there also seems to be growing over some religious bodies, despite the civilizing influences of our generation, an undue assumption of authority, whether as regards the individual conscience or men in general.

I, for one, assuredly quite feel and understand the necessity of a certain fixed and definite system of authoritative exposition, alike in matters of dogma and of doctrine. I equally assent to the unchanged need and the untold value of Creeds and Catechisms, and of the right- the absolute right, on every ground- of every religious body to lay down canons and directions for its own members, and even to assert and prescribe certain absolutely needful tests of teaching, either as articles of agreement or limits of orthodoxy.

But what I do not, and cannot understand, is why we should not all be content with this?

The Christian world is divided into irreconcilable sections at present. The unchristian world is torn by bitter and rival parties, and, therefore, to endeavor to enforce unity is alike hopeless and impracticable. But some good people there are who will never be content, unless they make you hold the same opinions they do! They may allege a love of the truth, of devotion to the church, whatever that church may be, as their leading and guiding principle of faith and action; but I confess, that I for one should much prefer that the golden law of "Caritas" governed a little more than it does do their expositions of belief and their efforts of duty. For the consequence is, that there is happening just now what is the inevitable outcome of such exaggerated views, and of such perversely fanatical teaching. The Church of Rome, not content with laying down rules of practice for her own members, is, by various allocutions and briefs, quietly excommunicating all Freemasons in particular countries *en bloc* and, in England itself, our loyal and peaceable and well-conducted order is openly accused by Roman Catholic and Reformed Presbyterian and Ritualistic writers of being indifferent to religion, antagonistic to truth, unsound and unbelieving, and Freemasonry generally is charged with being socialistic, revolutionary, and anarchical; a society hostile to good order and authority, and undeserving the support or approval of a Christian man! And when to these accusations we add the painful fact, that latterly a special and almost combined assault has been made on our peaceful and benevolent brotherhood by the heterogeneous and allied forces of Roman Catholicism, Reformed Presbyterianism, and Ritualistic Anglicanism, it would almost appear that the time has indeed come, when the glove thus hastily and hotly thrown down, should be taken up by some loyal defender of Freemasonry.

It is true that other attacks have been made on Freemasonry from time to time from various sources and from differing schools. Our good brethren in the United States have even had to go through the furnace of a long and open and cruel persecution; but, as a general rule, our assailants have been so contemptible, and their attacks so idle, that the good old craft has weathered grandly each successive storm. But at this hour, not only is an open Crusade being preached everywhere, apparently by order, against our harmless "Societas," but opinions are avowed, and objections are made, which seem to demand alike special notice and immediate reply. And, therefore, I have been induced to accept this quasi-challenge, and endeavor to make a response to the unreasoning fanaticism of our opponents, alike temperate in itself and not discreditable to Freemasonry.

For, I believe- I venture to do so- that by a calm examination of allegations and animadversions, put forward, too, with a great flourish of trumpets, I shall be able to demonstrate not only to an aggrieved fraternity, but even to some candid antagonists, how weak, after all, and harmless are the attacks of our heated adversaries; and how true, how fair, how consistent, how tolerant, how just, how good, is the actual position of our useful and philanthropic organization.

Leaving out of consideration, then, today, older attacks on our principles, and earlier assailants of Freemasonry, I will confine myself to a full examination of what may fairly be said, by any impartial writer, to be the main points of disapproval and condemnation, as publicly set forth, by writers of various schools of religious thought and teaching now. For if such hostile views prevail against our useful order, which I believe to be utterly unfounded in themselves, it is necessary to treat them in detail, and see wherein their error or misconception consists: and, on the other hand, as Freemasons, we are bound, on our own fair and tolerant principles, to give to all *bona fide* objectors and objections a patient and candid consideration. The main objections at the present time to Freemasonry seem to range themselves under two heads: 1stly, objections affecting its theory; and 2ndly, objections concerning its practice.

Under the first head necessarily are grouped : 1st, the accusation that Freemasonry is "only Theistical" in its constitution; 2ndly, that its avowed principles only inculcate bare morality; 3rdly, that it claims to be an "eclectic system" in itself, disregarding all other religious bodies; and 4thly, that its secrecy is objectionable, "per se," and equally on religious and on natural grounds.

Under the second head, objections are freely made: 1st, that it ignores Christianity and the name of a Savior; 2ndly, that it forms a spurious bond of union among men, and opposed to the true teaching of the Gospel; 3rdly, that in some countries, if not in England, it is a revolutionary society, and marked openly by socialistic and unbelieving views; 4thly, that it administers unlawful oaths; and 5thly, that it tends to excessive conviviality of habits.

There are, no doubt, other objections which have been made and still are made against Freemasonry, which, however, it would seem to be a pure waste of time to consider here, as they are either so trivial, or so evidently absurd in themselves, that our safest course, really and truly is, to pass them by in silence and contempt. But under these nine heads, I think the main allegations of our present adversaries are to be fairly found; and I am not without hope that, after a precise and careful examination of them one and all, on the good old principle of "audi alteram partem" some who may have too hastily endorsed or accepted the statements of the impugner, the caviller, and the calumniator, may be led to change their minds. And sure I am of this, that it can only be the fault or the weakness of him who thus seeks to defend the fur fame and true principles of his order, if all the efforts of credulity or hostility combined are able to loosen one stone in the broad and goodly foundation of the noble building of Freemasonry. I will commence, then, with the theoretical objections to Freemasonry.

I. First, its actual constitution is complained of that it is purely Theistical. It is said that a society which starts with the assumption that all men are admissible to its ranks, except the Atheist or the libertine, is not in accordance with the true position of a believer, of a Christian man!

Hence, some have said that Freemasonry is nothing but a Deistical body; that it is "Voltairean" that it is only "negatively religious," not "positively" and that the epoch of Theistical authority has passed away forever; and that no consistent Christian man can be a Freemason, because, on its own admission, it is defective in its actual constitution and theory.

Such seems to have been one old view of the Church of Rome (irrespective of any purely Roman theological objections); such appears to be the present opinion of the Reformed Presbyterian Synods of Glasgow and Edinburgh; and such also is the full-blown "presentment" of the Anglican Ritualistic writers and speakers at this very time.

For it is objected to Freemasonry, that by such teaching it puts practically all the religions in the world which admit and acknowledge the one Father of all, the Great Ruler of the World, on an equality, whether Christian or Non-christian; and that Christians are thus acting professedly and knowingly on certain common grounds of action and interest, with Hebrews, Hindus,

A DEFENSE OF FREEMASONRY

Parsees, Buddhists, and Mahommedans, while all Christian denominations are similarly welcome and recognized.

This objection, then, made of old, and repeated today, has to be met and dealt with, and I feel bound to say at once that I do not for one moment suppose that anything I can say on this "vexata quaestio," will remove the scruples of some, or give satisfaction to the complaints of others!

I would, however, venture to remind my readers that this position and this objection are alike inevitable from the very constitution of Freemasonry. Freemasonry being universal in its scope and organization, acts deliberately in thus enforcing and avowing its great and expansive system. Since 1813, the principles of Universalism, so to say, have been the great and distinguishing characteristic of the actual constitution and development of our Order in England.

And as most Freemasons rejoice in this width and breadth of Masonic action and progress, and consider it, and not unjustly, the one pre-eminent feature of their world-wide fraternity, I am anxious to impress on all who read these humble pages of mine, that, were Freemasonry to take a more circumscribed view, and to contract its platform, the great charm of its tolerant constitution would to many minds, I am sure, be at once taken utterly away.

For we must never forget, I venture to add, that Freemasonry embodies in its present constitution, in its actual profession, what is undoubtedly the divinest of all prayers, the recognition of an Universal Father of the human race. And though some might perhaps wish that the distinctive dogmas of Christianity were more fully admitted, or the leading principles of Christian teaching more openly avowed, yet, whether for good or for evil, the universality of Freemasonry is alike the representation of all its formularies and declarations, the key of its position, and the distinguishing token of its widespread brotherhood.

A DEFENSE OF FREEMASONRY

Some Masonic writers have liked to find a Christian and a mystical teaching in many a Masonic emblem, and many a lodge decoration, in explanations of our lectures, or portions of our ritual, and probably such a school will always exist in Freemasonry, and within due bounds has a good deal in it alike deserving of our attention and sympathy. But if such allusions may be found, and if such explanation may fairly be deduced, we can never lose sight of this one great fact as Freemasons, that that Ritual and these accessories, all the teaching, and all the traditions of the craft, are the common property of all our members, whatever their religious profession outside the Lodge may be.

When our opponents object to the broad platform of Freemasonry, and complain of Christians and Non-christians acting together for purposes of common benevolence and benefit of mankind, do they mean to contend that all such association is improper or inadvisable? If they do, they must at once, on their own principle, put a veto on all proceedings which tend by the aid of Christians and Non-christians, to administer help or relief to suffering man. And how, for instance, would such a state of things work in India? or how could such a principle be carried out in countries where Christianity is in the minority, and Non-christians have a large numerical preponderance?

This objection to Non-christians, if enforced, would put a stop to any possible combined movement for the succor and support of our fellow creatures, for the alleviation and removal of any of the griefs or sufferings which afflict our common humanity; but the truth is, the position of all such antagonists is entirely untenable in this respect. There is "no sectarianism in misery," as someone has well said, and there should be none in benevolence, sympathy, and mercy; and Freemasons in thus not refusing to associate themselves with all who, on one single and simple principle of cohesion and union can stand together and work together in the great cause of humanitarian goodwill and relief, are in my opinion most fully practicing the golden precept "honor all men." Let us all, in our several lots and positions, be as earnest religionists as we think right, but let us not overlook the feet, that two-thirds of the habitable world are as yet Non-christian, and to refuse to associate in any active labors with others, because they are Non-christian, especially in works of general utility and benevolence, reflects little credit on the spirit with which we seek to develop our own profession of true religion. Depend upon it, in this as in many other points, Freemasons are quite right, in thus making their test of admission as large and, universal, with two notable exceptions, as are the Masonic message of philanthropy and the Masonic sympathies of brotherhood.

Freemasonry knows nothing of distinctive dogmas or conflicting creeds, whether of Christian or Non-christian bodies, and welcomes them all, and has the same ritual for all, only sternly excluding the avowed Atheist, or the openly immoral man. I have always felt and feel today, that there is no use in blinking the difficulty, and that this objection may always form an insuperable bar to some earnest minds, and to some excellent men, and render Freemasonry less welcome or attractive to all such, than in my humble opinion, from its intrinsic excellency, it ever deserves to be.

For the earnest Christian- be he Romanist? or Anglican, or Reformed Presbyterian may say, I object to a society entirely, which is founded on such a basis and is equally tolerant of all, whether Christian or Non-christian, and cannot profess to form part of a brotherhood where heathen idolators, Mahommedans, or fire worshipers, and Christians and Hebrews all meet on the same level. But on the other hand, the Freemason may fairly ask, how can it be otherwise? the very essence of Freemasonry is its universality- the very glory of Freemasonry consists in its being a rallying point for men who differ, and differ widely, both in religion and politics. And, after all, the Freemason may argue, as the proverb says, "Half-a-loaf is better than none at all," and as even you Christians yourselves cannot meet together, or form one brotherhood, you should not despise in this day of "small things," our attempt to embody and put into practice, however imperfectly, what is in theory the teaching of Christianity proper, the "universal brotherhood of man."

For it is a very mistaken course for men to pursue here, though they often do it, because they cannot get all they want, to accept nothing at all, and inasmuch as Freemasonry does succeed in a marvelous manner; despite much opposition, many hard words, and more cavils, in bringing together happily and peacefully men of the most contrasted views and creeds, it surely deserves the hearty support of all who can elevate themselves above the limits of ecclesiastical or denominational teaching, and regard with kindly interest and sympathetic feeling their fellow creatures, their brother man.

I think it is the experience of all, it is my own after thirty-four years of Masonic membership, that the special charm of Freemasonry consists in this, that there is a spot where we forget the tumults and the troubles of the outer world, and where, retaining our own opinions modestly and manfully, we meet ever as brethren, and part ever as brethren, despite the differences which divide us, and the contentions which agitate us in social and public, and religious life. No doubt it may be said, such is also true of a Church, or House of God in our land, where His people can assemble together, and forget alike earthly sorrow and worldly distractions, and such certainly is so. But while those who meet in the church are mostly of the same creed outwardly at any rate, in a lodge-room the utmost diversity prevails ever, both of religious belief and of political party. Yet is it not often a strange metamorphosis which our Masonic Lodge gatherings can effect on us antagonistic mortals now?

Outside its portals we are members of the community, supporters of the Church, members of a denominational body, citizens of the world, each with our own pet theories, and probably discordant aspirations. Inside that room, however humble, a spell has come over us. We are all one, one in peaceful unity and brotherly concord, one in goodwill to our fellowmen, one in giving glory to our Common Father in Heaven.

As Freemasons, we may be wrong in all this. We may not come up to what some think should be the proper formulae of our religious profession; but to this very system we owe, many of us, nay, I will say all of us, some of the happiest and cheeriest moments of our lives, some of our fastest friendships; and some of our most refreshing memories. Whatever else may betide Freemasonry; whatever attacks it may have to endure; whatever condemnation to face; it never can give up its universality, without, as it were, loosening the capstone of that great arch which spans in its tolerating brotherhood all those of our human race, who, with us, acknowledge and bow down reverently before the Great Architect of the world, and the one loving Father of mankind.

If Freemasonry has to be condemned because it is, then, Theistical, admitting and welcoming all religious denominations, and all bodies of men, Christian or Non-christian who believe simply in God Most High, Freemasonry will have to be condemned. Nothing, I feel sure, will ever induce Freemasons to falter for one moment in the avowal of its universal teaching; and nothing I fear that I can say, will remove the scruples of those, who find the broad platform of Masonic brotherhood the great stumbling-block to their approval of its principles, and the standing-ground for complaint, anathema, and condemnation.

It is impossible to argue out such a subject with those with whom we cannot agree on first principles, and therefore I leave it here, believing that by the fair, the tolerant, and the liberal-minded, the position which Freemasonry assumes in this respect, will be alike appreciated and approved.

A DEFENSE OF FREEMASONRY

II. When we come to the second article of accusation, namely, "the inculcation of bare morality," the true Freemason will smile, and the champion of Freemasonry will find his work neither serious nor difficult, for a more absurd charge was never brought by a sentient being against our good old order. Freemasonry being universal, as I have already pointed out, in its acceptation of all beliefs and denominations, with the two exceptions to which I have so frequently adverted, that I need hardly repeat them now, has, of course, no creed or catechism to propound to its affiliated members. Good as they are, and necessary as they may be deemed to religious communities, they are, and would be, altogether out of place in Freemasonry. For as Freemasonry is not, nor does it profess to be a religion to any one, nor even to inculcate, except indirectly, religious truth, it has no dogmas to assert; no terms of communion to enforce. But it does what it can do fitly and honestly; it accepts God's Inspired Word as the one true teaching of moral duty and personal responsibility, and it recommends all its members urgently to regulate alike their slightest words and actions by the Divine precepts the Best of Books contains. Indeed, I know of no place on earth, outside the Church of course, where so much simple reverence is paid to God's Word, as in our Masonic lodges, and if the morality of the Bible can be called "bare morality," then no doubt the moral and binding obligations which Freemasonry ever recognizes and inculcates must be styled "bare morality" too.

But if the morality of God's own directing and controlling Word be true and right, so equally is that of our Masonic lore; for it is none other from first to last in every warning, in every exhortation, in every injunction, than what is to be found clearly set down in the pages of Holy Writ. Some, no doubt, object to teach, as they say, morality without belief, and practice without dogma; but that condition of things, however befitting purely religious organizations, is utterly impossible in Freemasonry, owing to its universal formularies of discipline and doctrine.

A DEFENSE OF FREEMASONRY

For it would indeed be hopeless, (to say nothing of the unfairness or impropriety,) to attempt to enforce under the semblance of a philanthropic fraternity, Christian teaching on the Hebrew, or Hindu, or Mahommedan, and therefore, we simply appeal to God's Word, and make it, in this country, happily, still ever at any rate the one standard for us all alike of moral conduct and of moral certainty. And what more can we do?

In so acting consistently and habitually, though not religion, as I before contended, Freemasonry becomes a handmaid to religion. For as claiming and accepting "bona fide" that blessed Book on which the whole superstructure of Christianity itself is built up, as its one sacred and solemn authority, alike for general duties and personal practice, it can associate itself with all willingly, in common labors of love and benevolence, who, without raising the question of this test, or elevating the shibboleth of that dogma, are willing to seek to conform to, and carry out in practical beneficence the one unchanging moral law of our Heavenly Father and Teacher.

It was said once upon a time by Him who spake alone as never man spake here below, "He that is not against us is on our part," and I for one, have always greatly regretted and deprecated the difficulties which many good and conscientious persons have found on this point; difficulties winch appear to me to exist more in apprehension than in reality.

Far wiser and better is it, I venture humbly to conceive and to say today, for all religious bodies not to antagonize or condemn Freemasonry, simply because while it accepts "ex animo" the great Charter of all Christian life, liberty, and law, it cannot, from its very position enforce or adopt as binding on its multifarious members the creed of this Christian Church, or the catechism of that religious denomination.

Some one has called Freemasonry a religion of morality,

and so perhaps, in accordance with our own formularies, it may be termed, but on the whole I think it better to adhere to what has ever appeared to me the truest and safest teaching of all our ablest writers, namely, that Freemasonry is one universal and benevolent brotherhood, ignoring altogether sectarian differences of opinion, but promulgating ever most distinctly, the Bible lessons of morality and duty and responsibility.

Freemasonry has also to encounter in its onward career the animad-versions of those who object to the Bible being used in the lodges at all.

In many of the foreign lodges- in France, Belgium, etc- the Bible is never authoritatively introduced, and any allusion to the Bible as the true source of all moral teaching, and the inspired witness of all moral duty, is looked upon as either a proof of superstition or even of intolerance, though by what possible argument this "intolerance" of "Bibliolatry," as it has been termed, can be upheld, I know not. The only intolerance that I am aware of is that of the free thinker, the "esprit libre."

The rank Infidel who, objecting naturally to the Bible, seeks to deprive his brethren, who love it and value it, and look to it as the sacred sanction of every Masonic virtue and all Masonic labors, the great and directing light of Freemasonry in fact, he is assuredly most intolerant.

Sad is it to see in what a dismal and dangerous morass many have lost their way, and seem hopelessly sunk abroad, who have preferred the deceiving "Will-o'-the-wisps" of mundane philosophy to the purer and clearer rays of God's own truth.

To them this world is still a "chaos," and we all poor struggling "atoms" in a mighty aggregate, here today and gone tomorrow, our only goal utter annihilation, our only future an endless sleep. Alas for all who take up with the destructive theories of modern philosophical unbelief. Any who venture to seek to deprive their brethren of the "droit de croire," will only succeed in reducing Freemasonry to the absolute negation of all revealed truth, or to the unsatisfactory condition of a semi-stoical and semi-pantheistic school, without consistency, logic, or reality.

We in England, keeping the golden mean, intend- I speak for many Freemasons like myself- never to let go that religious position which our Freemasonry has ever assumed, and which, though universal in its profession and practice, ever carefully preserves and faithfully cherishes as the great light of all lodges the revered volume of the sacred law, the one unerring standard of right and wrong.

But it may be as well to lay down here what we do really teach as regards moral duty; and I cannot do better than make use of the following eloquent words of an old Masonic writer:

"First, then, our Order instructs us in our duty to the great Artificer of the universe; directs us to behave as becomes creatures to their Creator; to be satisfied with His dispensations, and always to rely upon Him whose wisdom cannot mistake our happiness, whose goodness cannot contradict it. It directs us to be peaceable subjects, to give no umbrage to the civil powers, and never to be concerned in plots and conspiracies against the well-being of the nation; and as political matters have sown the seeds of discord among the nearest relations and most intimate friends, we are wisely enjoined in our assemblies never to speak of them. It instructs us in our duty to our neighbor; teaches us to injure him in none of his connections, and in all our dealings with him to act with justice and impartiality. It discourages defamation; it bids us not to circulate any whisper of infamy, improve any hint of suspicion, or publish any failure of conduct. It orders us to be faithful to our trusts; to deceive not him who relieth upon us; to be above the meanness of dissimulation; to let the words of our mouths be the thoughts of our hearts, and whatsoever we promise religiously to perform. It teaches inviolable secrecy; forbids us to discover our mystic rites to the unenlightened, or to betray the confidence of a brother. It warms our hearts with true philanthropy, with that philanthropy which directs us never to permit a wretched fellow-creature to pass by till we have presented him with the cup of consolation, and have made him drink copious draughts of the heart-reviving milk of human kindness. It makes us lovers of order; stifles enmity, wrath, and dissension, and nourishes love, peace, friendship, and every social virtue; it tells us to seek our happiness in the happiness we bestow, and to love our neighbor as ourselves. It informs us that we are all children of one father; that man is an infirm, short-lived creature, who passes away like a shadow; that he is hastening to that place where human titles and distinctions are not considered; where the trappings of pride will be taken away, and virtue alone have the pre-eminence; and thus instructed, we profess that merit is the only proper distinction. We are not to vaunt ourselves upon our riches or our honors, but to clothe ourselves with humility; to condescend to men of low estate; to be the friends of merit in whatever rank we find it. We are connected with men of the most indigent circumstances, and in a lodge, (though our Order deprives no man of the honor due to his dignity or character,) we rank as brethren on a level; and out of a lodge, the most abject wretch we behold belongs to the great fraternity of mankind; and therefore, when it is in our power, it is our duty to support the distressed, and patronize the neglected. It directs us to divest ourselves of confined and bigoted notions, (the source of so many cruel persecutions,) and teaches us that humanity is the soul of all religions. We never suffer any religious disputes in our lodges, (such disputes tend to disturb the tranquility of the mind,) and as Masons, we believe that in every nation he that feareth Him and worketh righteousness, is accepted of Him. All Masons, therefore, whether Christians, Jews, or Mahommedans, who violate not the rule of right written by the Almighty upon the tablets of the heart, who do fear Him, and work righteousness, we are to acknowledge as brethren; and though we take different roads, we are not to be angry with each other on that account; we mean all to travel to the same place; we know that the end of our journey is the same; and we are all affectionately to hope to meet in the lodge of perfect happiness. How lovely is an institution fraught with sentiments like these; how agreeable must it be to Him who is seated on a throne of everlasting mercy; to that God who is no respecter of persons."

"It instincts us likewise in our duty to ourselves; it teaches us to set just bounds to our desires; to put a curb upon our sensual appetites; to walk uprightly. Our Order excludes women; not because it is unwilling we should pay a proper regard to that lovely sex, the greatest, the most valuable gift that heaven has bestowed upon us, but it bids us enjoy their society in such a manner as the laws of conscience, sobriety, and temperance, permit. It commands us for momentary gratifications not to destroy the peace of families; not to take away the happiness, (a happiness with which grandeur and riches are not to be compared,) which those experience whose hearts are united by love; not to profane the first and most holy institution of nature. To enjoy the blessings sent by divine beneficence, he tells us, in virtue and obedience; but it bids us avoid the allurements of intemperance, whose short hours of jollity are followed by tedious days of pain and dejection; whose days turn to madness, and lead to diseases and to death. Such are the duties which our Order teaches us, and Masonry (the heavenly genius!) seems now thus to address us. The Order I have established in every part of it shows consummate wisdom; founded on moral and social virtue, it is supported by strength; it is adorned by beauty/ for everything is found in it that can make society agreeable. In the most striking manner I teach you to act with propriety in every station of life. The tools and implements of architecture, and everything about you, I have contrived to be most expressive symbols to convey to you the strongest moral truths. Let your improvement be proportionate to your instruction. Be not contented with the name only of Freemasons. Invested with my ancient and honorable badge, be masons indeed. Think not that it is to be so to meet together, and to go through the ceremonies which I have appointed; these ceremonies, in such an Order as mine, are necessary, but they are the most immaterial part of it, and there are weightier matters which you must not omit. To be Masons indeed, is to put in practice the lessons of wisdom which I teach you. With reverential gratitude, therefore, cheerfully worship the Eternal Providence; bow down yourselves in filial and submissive obedience to the unerring direction of the Mighty Builder; work by His perfect plans, and your edifices shall be beautiful and everlasting. I command you to love your neighbor; stretch forth the hand of relief to him if he be in necessity; if he be in danger, run to his assistance; tell him the truth if he be deceived; if he be unjustly reproached and neglected, comfort his soul, and soothe it to tranquility. You cannot show your gratitude to your Creator in a more amiable light, than in your mutual regard for each other. Taught as you are by me to root out bigoted notions, have charity for the religious sentiments of all mankind; nor think the mercies of the Father of all the families of the earth, of that Being whom the heaven of heavens cannot contain, are confined within the narrow limits of any particular sect or religion."

"Pride not yourselves upon your birth- it is of no consequence of what parents any man is born, provided he be a man of merit; nor your honors, they are the objects of envy and impertinence, and must ere long be laid in the dust; nor your riches, they cannot gratify the wants they create; but be meek, and lowly of heart. I reduce all conditions to a pleasing and rational equality; pride was not made for man, and he that humbleth himself shall be exalted. I am not gloomy and austere. I am a preacher of morality, but not a gloomy and severe one; for I strive to render it lovely to you by the charms of pleasures which leave no sting behind; by moral music, rational joy, and harmless gaiety. I bid you not to abstain from the pleasures of society, or innocent enjoyments; to abstain from them is to frustrate the intentions of Providence. I enjoin you not to consecrate your hours to solitude.

A DEFENSE OF FREEMASONRY

Society is the true sphere of human virtue; and no life can be pleasing to God but what is useful to man. On every festival, in which well-pleased, my sons, I see you assembled to honor me, be happy. Let no pensive look profane the general joy; let sorrow cease; let none be wretched; and let pleasure and her bosom friends, attend this social board. Pleasure is a stranger to every malignant and unsocial passion, and is formed to expand, to exhilarate, to humanize the heart. But he is not to be met with at the table of turbulent festivity; he disclaims all connections with indecency and excess, and declines the society of riot roaring in the jollity of his heart. A sense of the dignity of human nature always accompanies him, and he admits not of anything that degrades it. Temperance and cheerfulness are his bosom friends; and at the social board, where he never refuses his presence, these friends are always placed on his right hand and on his left; during the time he generally addresses himself to cheerfulness, till intemperance demands his attention. On your festivals, I say, be happy; but remember now, and always remember, you are Masons, and act in such a manner that the eyes of the censorious, ever fixed upon you, may see nothing in your conduct worthy of reproof; the tongue of the slanderer, always ready to revile you, may be put to silence. Be models of virtue to mankind. Examples profit more than precepts. Lead uncorrupt lives, do the thing which is right and speak the truth from your hearts. Slander not your neighbor, and do no other evil unto him; and let your good actions convince the world of the wisdom and advantages of my institution. The unworthiness of some of those who have been initiated into my Order, but who have not made themselves acquainted with me, and who, because I am a friend to rational gaiety, have ignorantly thought excesses might be indulged in, has been disgraceful to themselves and discreditable to me."

Such, surely, is teaching, alike simple and consistent and true, creditable to Freemasonry and beneficial to mankind.

III. A third allegation against; Freemasonry is, that it

professes to be an eclectic system in itself, disregarding all other philosophies, and even all other religions!

I was not aware until this statement was made by a recent impugner alike of the constitution and teaching and practice of Freemasonry, that any English Masonic writer of any authority had ever said anything in defense of, or in illustration of Freemasonry, to justify such a complaint.

In Great Britain, and I believe, in America, Freemasons have never adopted any other view of Freemasonry, as far as I know, than the one to which I have so lately drawn attention under the second head of theoretical objections, viz., that Freemasonry was a world-wide philanthropic confraternity, overlooking denominationalism, to use a common form of expression just now, but advocating moral duty and practical benevolence. But I am equally aware of the fact that in foreign countries, theories of Freemasonry have been propounded which serve to give a color to this objection.

Some foreign Masonic writers, in past times and the present, animated honestly by strong humanitarian yearnings, have liked to look at and describe Freemasonry as a great moral philosophy of right and civilization, toleration, and elevation, as well as an ennobling and admirable school of self-culture and self-discipline; and within certain recognized limits, such views of Freemasonry are not unfounded. For Freemasonry does, undoubtedly, in the calm teaching of moral duty and responsibility with which it invests all its esoteric lore from first to last, in its great and immutable principles of justice and sincerity, of trust and toleration, of largeness of thought and freedom of conscience, Freemasonry, does, I say, present to the eye of all its admiring children, a reality of practical teaching deeply important and needful to us all alike in our onward progress through life. But when in the fervor of their philosophic aspirations, or in the excess of their Masonic zeal, such enthusiastic brethren, whether the neophyte or the veteran, seek to give to Freemasonry the character of a self existing and independent school of thought or, "academe" of philosophy, or even of a religion to the world and to its initiates, they resemble only in so doing one of old who made himself wings of wax which melted before the sun's fiery rays, so that he could not fly but fell to the ground!

For, however excellent and praiseworthy Freemasonry is in itself, whether we have regard to its symbolism or its ritualism, its ancient traditions or its mystical applications, its unceasing exhortations to self-knowledge and moral restraint, it must ever inevitably fail if it assumes the status of a religion, or professes to be religion to the mind and conscience of man.

No doubt in some Continental countries, where Freemasonry has been until lately all but proscribed, and still has a hard struggle for existence, where it has an hourly encounter to expect, and an hourly combat to wage with many and irreconcilable enemies, there is a tendency, almost unavoidable from the state of things, to exalt the noble axioms and moral truths of Freemasonry into the rank of positive and religious teaching, or into an eclectic school of philosophy and even of belief, in order to obtain, so to say, a "locus standi" against vehement adversaries, and amid unending strife.

But such is not necessarily the true exposition of the meaning and mission of Freemasonry, neither is such an enlarged theory of Masonic teaching held in any degree, I believe, among Anglo-Saxon Freemasons.

I for one, and I believe many more heartily agree with me, do not profess to sympathize with those writers, however able or well-intentioned, who strive, as I view it, to raise Freemasonry, to its permanent injury, above its true level, whether as a Brotherhood or a system.

A DEFENSE OF FREEMASONRY

To some, indeed, Freemasonry from its many and increasing claims on their reverence and attachment, especially where its peaceful and tolerant principles are openly denounced and condemned, may stand, "in loco religionis," as they say, but they are the exception to the rule, even in those very countries, and are very few and far between indeed, in our own country and in the United States.

I feel that I should not be doing my duty to my brethren if I did not carefully point out how unwarranted and mistaken such an explanation of Freemasonry is, and how prejudicial it may become, if too much insisted on, to the rightful claim of Freemasonry, both on our sympathies and devotion. Greatly, indeed, in my humble opinion, would Freemasonry suffer if by any outburst of Masonic enthusiasm, we should any of us endeavor to elevate it to a position or character it was never intended clearly to uphold or to assume.

And if there is one warning which experience would give us, it is this- never, in our contests or contact with the world outside, or with secular combatants, be they who they may, to put forward excessive claims, or to rest upon untenable assumptions. The harm we shall do to our useful and admirable institution will be irreparable, believe me, if either through a too hasty induction, or by a careless assent to ill-digested opinions, we assign to Freemasonry attributes and qualities, and features and tendencies of thought and practice which do not really belong to it, and which, if they did really correctly describe its first or even its second principles, must assuredly retard its mission and hinder its progress among mankind.

While, then, the "eclectic" representation of Freemasonry I admit is to be found in some foreign writers and writings, we have not adopted it and we know nothing of it in English Freemasonry. A Masonic writer, for instance, has lately said in one of our publications: I confess, the following, which I take from a

A DEFENSE OF FREEMASONRY

German Masonic paper, "Bauhutte," is somewhat staggering, and goes a good way to make one believe that continental Masonry is something very different from the mere good fellowship, and sociality combined with benevolence, which are generally accepted as the characteristics of the order in England:

"Protestantism, unable to extricate itself from that slavish subjection to the letter as opposed to the spirit in which it remains hopelessly embedded as in a quicksand, and lacking completely all the motive power of a vigorous and progressive intellectual life, has of itself crumbled away into multitudinous sects, all utterly powerless against others and divided among themselves, so that now it can be considered only in the light of a dead letter. The only existing real and vital power is United Catholic Christendom, welded into one body by Jesuit influence. This acts as a formidable drag to the wheels of progress, and as a barrier to the development and enlightenment of the human race, and as such must be regarded by all Freemasons who have the interests of our League near at heart. He who would win largely must stake high. According to the dictum of the Church, which styles itself Roman, Catholic, Papal, and Infallible, every Freemason must, *ipso facto*, cease to be a Christian. This Church is supremely hostile, not only to Freemasonry, but to all associations whose aim is to spread enlightenment and civilization. If, therefore, we desire to be true Freemason, and to further the cause, to the advancement of which we have pledged ourselves, we must without reserve or hesitation adopt as our own the words of Strauss, and proclaim aloud: 'We are no longer Christians, we are simply Freemasons; nothing less and nothing more.' We must concentrate all our powers to effect the one thing necessary- to unite all mankind in the bond of a common humanity. Mere dilettantism in Freemasonry can never be of real service to the human race, nor win for the Brotherhood real respect. The present time is not one of compromise; let us refuse to carry a doubtful banner."

To such views English Freemasons cannot subscribe, and

we very much doubt whether they are held by a majority of the German Freemasons. The Spanish Grand Lodge has lately this very year put oat a sort of manifesto, and an eloquent defense of Freemasonry. But in it occur passages which serve to give color to the allegations of our adversaries, that Freemasonry seeks to raise itself to the rank of a religion for mankind! For it mentions, first of all, those improvements and changes which advancing time brings to the world and man, such as progress and civilization, science and material well-being, intellectual knowledge, love, fraternity, equality, liberty, all the virtues, the richest treasures of the human heart, which are yet to be sown broadcast over the earth in order to arrive at perfectibility. At the same time the manifesto goes on to say, are to be witnessed the downfall of error and ignorance, the annihilation of fanaticism and barbarism, hatred and fear are both to disappear, as well as the dim and alarming veil of the future, which magically will fall back before us.

And Freemasonry is to do all this, as the advanced sentinel of such civilization, as the invincible phalanx of progress and decided champion of these virtues; it is a sublime institution; nay, with somewhat of immortality.

As ancient as the world, and, as the world, it has unceasingly labored in all places and in all times to implant in the heart of man the generous seed of good. It holds ever to love and fraternity as its main principles; its end is the perfection of man; and as means to attain to such bliss it puts forward union, equality, justice, and the incomparable morality of its sublime teaching. But in order that Freemasonry may eventually reach to the happy termination of its most sacred mission, that in its midst humanity shall regenerate itself, and thought be emancipated, that the light of reason, and of truth shall luminously irradiate human ideas, that moral and material progress may become a fact, it is necessary that we learn not only to realize the importance of unity, but to abandon those contests which give rise to severances, which so prejudice any institution, to divest ourselves of their miseries, and their bastard passions. And becoming, grand, powerful, united by the firm bonds of love and fraternity, let us march on joined together for one good, guarded by the same will, faithful to the same idea.

Now this, though all very pretty writing, and marked by the sonorousness of the proverbial Spanish power of words, is not a true representation of Freemasonry according to our calmer ideas, rather it is a representation in "excess."

Curiously enough, there was issued in 1869, a statement of the aims and objects of Freemasonry by the Portuguese Masons, and making some allowance for the vivacity of our foreign brethren, which sometimes seems to jar a little on our more measured and sober manner of expression, and more moderate and careful limits of thought, is to be commended and accepted by us.

"Freemasonry is a great association of men who have made it their task to live in perfect equality, intimately united by the bonds of mutual confidence, mutual esteem, and friendship, under the name of brothers- the sweetest and truest appellation they could attribute to themselves- and to stimulate each other to the practice of benevolence and morality. Freemasonry is great in the eyes of the generous, good, and honest; it is nothing to the narrow-minded, the wicked, the faithless. It is sublime, it is everything to the wise and virtuous; it is nothing to the ambitious, the covetous, the false. It is great to the sensible man, the sincere,and the generous, who is conscious of the infirmities of man, and who feels the obligation of healing them. Freemasonry is neither a conspiracy nor a party affair; it neither serves ambition nor deceit. It is order and truth in all things. It hates all vices, it loves every virtue, it is the Godly voice which calleth upon us to love and help each other. It is tranquility in storms, a beacon in shipwreck, consolation in misfortune; it is, in a word, the true union of nations. Freemasonry is august; it is everything to those who comprehend it, it is nothing to those whose heart and soul are dead. Freemasonry is an institution which allows no doubt, no contest as to its principles. It is the purest and simplest of all institutions. Its principles are such as to agree best with that reason so liberally bestowed on us by the G.A.O.T.U. Freemasonry is neither a religious sect nor a political party; it embraces, however, all parties, all sects, in order to unite all its disciples in one common brotherhood. Freemasonry is the touchstone for every truth. It is the torch of reason, serving to distinguish good from evil, truth from falsehood, courage from cowardice, and generosity from selfishness. It teaches us to conquer the obstacles which ignorance, fanaticism, and prejudice oppose to it."

I think too that the true position of Freemasonry in this respect is so well expressed in the able essay of an American writer, that I add it to this portion of my defense:

"Masonry does not claim for itself a divine origin. It does not claim to be a religious institution in any strict sense, but it recognizes the existence of a Supreme Euler of the universe, and makes a belief in Him a moral and religious test of admission into its lodges. It teaches morality, friendship, brotherly love, 'faith in God, hope in immortality, and charity to all,' but it does not assume to usurp the prerogative of the Church or the offices of the Ministry. It has no sympathy with that spirit that opposes or ridicules the Church, or seeks to exalt any society or system of philanthropy above religion. Our laws contemplate that no Atheist, either practical or speculative, should ever cross the threshold of a lodge. While our Order can hold no affiliation with sects, and while we accord to every man, of whatever creed, freedom of opinion, Masonic toleration can go no further. That man is not fit material for a Masonic edifice who denies the existence of God, of a personal God, who created all things, and who reigns the Sovereign Ruler of all created things. It is impossible for such a man to become a true Mason, because he would not be bound by moral obligations, or subject to moral restraints, The Fraternity would have no adequate guarantee that he would keep the moral law, or perform the obligation or duties assumed by Masons. The great incentive to rectitude would be lacking, moral principle wanting, and his conduct dictated by convenience, self-interest, passion, prejudice or fear. His attachment to the Order would be a pretense; his participation in its work a form, and his daily life a reproach upon the Order. Such a man would lack the true incentive to efforts to promote the common good or general happiness, and would be unworthy of the confidence of his brethren, without which there could be no true union, no real fraternity."

"The true Mason is taught to reverence God, and to look upon the duties enjoined upon him by Masonry as such, because they are enjoined by His revealed will, or are plainly in accord with His moral Government. He is taught that neither convenience, pleasure, self-interest, passion, or prejudice, is to swerve him from the path of duty. Masonry thus becomes a mighty power for the improvement of the human race. It aggregates the influence, contributions, and labors of its numerous votaries in systematic efforts to teach the world the great lessons of charity, spread the light of knowledge, and in short, to bring mankind up to that position of social excellence demanded by the purest morality. 'It wields the great moral forces of Faith, Hope, and Charity for the regeneration of the race.' Another no less important qualification for a candidate for Masonry is a belief in the immortality of the soul. Without this belief the moral law would possess no adequate sanction, and the most beautiful allegories and symbols of our Order would be meaningless. Masonry writes over her portals not the infidel motto, placed over the entrance to the cemeteries of France during the Revolution, 'Death is an eternal sleep;' but the motto of Masonry is, 'The soul is immortal.' She consigns the mortal part of a deceased brother to the grave, but plants there the emblem of immortality, in faith that that which 'is sown in corruption' will be raised in 'incorruption,' and that the soul, the immortal part, will shine forth a living stone in that temple 'not made with hands, eternal in the heavens.' But not only must a candidate for Masonry believe in the existence of God and the immortality of the soul, but every candidate for admission into the fraternity must be obedient to the moral law; not simply to the Decalogue, but to that law of good and evil inscribed upon man's conscience by the Creator- a rule alike binding upon every man by divine authority, and of universal obligation among all nations, tongues and creeds. Masonry has been well defined to be the 'universal morality which is suited to the inhabitants of every clime, to the men of every creed.'"

Brother James Rolfe, writing in 1857 in the old "Freemason's Magazine," asks and answers admirably the question, "What is Free- masonry?"

"On the threshold of the inquiry let us pause a moment to ask, 'What is Masonry?' and I think no better answer can be given than that which she herself puts in the mouth of her neophytes- 'A peculiar system of morality veiled in allegory, and illustrated by symbols.' We may style her what she really is- the sister of science, the handmaid of religion, the standard and watchword round which men of every politics and sects may rally, the neutral ground of the polemic; the haven of refuge to the faint-hearted and weary; the measure of leaven acting upon the whole mass of society; but after all we must recur to her own strict and logical definition of herself, wherein she declares that she is a system of morals, claiming, therefore, attention from the well-disposed and the pious; that she is veiled in allegory, that men may inquire into her, ponder over her, and, not deeming that she is to be lightly wooed and won with ease, must devote to her reflection, earnestness, and zeal; illustrated by symbols that the outward aspect of nature and the creations of industry and art may ever recall to the Masonic mind a sense of its intrinsic nobility and eternity, and that almost every object which meets our gaze should remind us of those laws which Masonry would have us take for our guide whilst passing through this outer porch- the world; waiting carefully and hopefully till we be admitted within the entrance of the Holiest of Holies. That Masonry, founded in such a remote antiquity, should have endured so many thousand years unaltered amid the rise and fall of empires; that the flow of civilization should not have dispersed her, nor the ebbing of its tide overwhelmed her; that she has revived alike in the refinement, grandeur, and intelligence of a capital, and in the solitude and barbarism of a desert; that she has been preserved dear as the memory of home and fatherland in the desolation of captivity; and that, after a lapse of fifty centuries, she ranges beneath her banner a larger and goodlier host than at any preceding period of her history- all this is not only a glory to her in itself, but is a proof beyond denial that she is built on a rock, her foundation sound, her structure well compacted, and that she is the most perfect of merely human institutions. The disappointed, the unjust, and the cynic may deny the existence of human sympathies and affections, and may style them the Utopia of the poet, the dream of the young, and the delusion of the simple; but on the consecrated ground of a Mason's lodge, I would say, does not Masonry tell us that these are the realities? and, like a winnowing fan, diffuse the husk and dross till the pure grain alone remains. Does she not, like a wise and careful mother, appeal to the best feelings of our nature, and strive by cultivation of them to destroy in us whatever is base, and vile, and low? For which purpose she has laid down for her principles truth, brotherly love, and belief- Truth, viz., the written and unwritten Law of Jehovah in the inspired contents of the volume of the Sacred Law; and in the aspirations and intuitions of that soul which was breathed into man by the Most High. Truth absolute and intact- 1st, as regards the Giver of the law; 2nd, as regards the law itself; and, 3rd, as the rule of Masonic life. Masonry can no more exist without truth than we can without the food we eat or the air we breathe. It is the cement which binds together the whole fabric of Masonry; and when an individual ceases to regard truth he is no longer a Mason, for Masonry is of the heart and inner life, and if truth should be tampered with by Masonry herself, her days would be numbered and her destruction nigh."

"Brotherly love- because it is the essence of every scheme

of religion and every system of morality; and what is Masonry but brotherly love! It is the ethos of the Greek, the charity of the Christian, and the distinguishing and pre-eminent quality of the Great God, the test and proof of our nearness to Him. It is to think no guile, to speak no evil, to do no wrong to any one in the world, to enwrap our brother in our sympathies as in a thick cloud, to shelter him from the blight of calumny, to ward off the attacks of the open enemy and the insidious foe. It is the great corrective against all that is base, mean, and selfish. It teaches that man does not live for himself alone; that, as a member of society, he has many spheres of duty which can be faithfully discharged only in the spirit of charity. It has its blessings and reward here in the gratitude of those on whom its gentle influence has fallen as the sunbeam on the ripening grain, or the dew on the droughty earth; in the love of those with whom its life is spent; and in the respect of the wise and good. And hereafter, eternal as the God from whom it sprang, it will be perfected in the realms of everlasting love, and form the burden of that glowing strain, and the key-note of that surpassing harmony, which shall resound through the universe for ever. And that we should not confine ourselves to any theory, however sublime, she lays her foundation on relief- not only that almsgiving which affects the purse, but such a relief as time, labor, thought, self-sacrifice, and inconvenience can bestow on our less fortunate fellow-creatures. She knows that the active discharge of every-day duties best forms the characters which belong to those who profess her doctrines, and that those who best fulfill those kindly offices will gain the keenest insight into her mysteries. And so, whilst worshiping the sanctity of Truth, and nourishing, as it were, our whole spiritual being on brotherly love, she bids us do justly and love mercy. Is it wonderful that, built on such a foundation, Masonry has endured so long! Is it not, rather, certain that, if her sons be true to her, Masonry will not cease from the earth till the G.A.O.T.U. shall bid the new creation rise from the ruins of the lower world?"

I think it also well here to remind my readers of the

authoritative teaching of our order in this respect.

"A Mason is obliged, by his tenure, to obey the moral law; and if he rightly understand the art he will never be a stupid Atheist or an irreligious libertine. He, of all men, should best understand that God seeth not as man seeth; for man looketh at the outward appearance, but God looketh to the heart. A Mason, is, therefore, particularly bound never to act against the dictates of his conscience. Let a man's religion or mode of worship be what it may, he is not excluded from the Order, provided he believe in the glorious Architect of Heaven and earth, and practice the sacred duties of morality. Masons unite with the virtuous of every persuasion in the firm and pleasing bond of fraternal love; they are taught to view the errors of mankind with compassion, and to strive, by the purity of their own conduct, to demonstrate the superior excellence of the faith they may process. Thus Masonry is the center of union between good men and true, and the happy means of conciliating friendship among those who must otherwise have remained at a perpetual distance. A Mason is a peaceable subject to the civil powers wherever he resides or works, and is never to be concerned in plots and conspiracies against the peace and welfare of the nation, nor to behave himself undutifully to inferior magistrates. He is cheerfully to conform to every lawful authority; to uphold, on every occasion, the interest of the community, and zealously promote the prosperity of his own country. Masonry has ever flourished in times of peace, and been always injured by war, bloodshed, and confusion; so that kings and princes, in every age, have been much disposed to encourage the Craftsmen on account of their peaceableness and loyalty, whereby they practically answer the cavils of their adversaries, and promote the honor of the fraternity. Craftsmen are bound by peculiar ties to promote peace, cultivate harmony, and live in concord and brotherly love."

Bros. Dr. Oliver and Jethro Inwood have also well said: "Freemasonry is neither an exclusive system of religion, nor does it tolerate the detestable principles of infidelity. All the plans and ceremonies of Freemasonry are pacific. It breathes nothing but the spirit of love and charity to all mankind. It cooperates with true religion in regulating the tempers, in restraining the passions, and harmonizing the discordant interests of men. In one hand it holds the olive-branch of peace; in the other, the liberal offerings of universal charity. The distinguishing characteristic of our institution is charity in its most ample sense- that charity, which has been justly described as the chief of ail the social virtues. Charity has been thus beautifully defined by Preston:

'This virtue includes a supreme degree of love to the great Creator and Governor of the universe, and an unlimited affection to the beings of His creation, of all characters and of every denomination. This last duty is forcibly inculcated by the example of the Deity Himself, who liberally dispenses his beneficence to unnumbered worlds. It is not particularly our province to enter into a disquisition of every branch of this amiable virtue; we shall, therefore, only briefly state the happy effects of a benevolent disposition toward mankind, and show that charity, exerted on proper objects, is the greatest pleasure man can possibly enjoy. The bounds of the greatest nation, or the most extensive empire, cannot circumscribe the generosity of a liberal mind. Men, in whatever situation they are placed, are still, in a great measure the same. They are exposed to similar dangers and misfortunes j they have not wisdom to foresee, or power to prevent, the evils incident to human nature; they hang, as it were, in a perpetual suspense between hope and fear, sickness and health, plenty and want. A mutual chain of dependence subsists throughout the animal creation. All of the human species are, therefore, proper objects for the exercise of charity. Beings who partake of one common nature ought to be actuated by the same motives and interests. Hence, to soothe the unhappy by sympathizing with their misfortunes, and to restore peace and tranquility to agitated spirits, constitute the general and great ends of the Masonic system. This humane, this generous disposition, fires the breast with manly feelings, and enlivens that spirit of compassion which is the glory of the human frame, and which not only rivals, but outshines every other pleasure that the mind is capable of enjoying. All human passions, when directed by the superior principle of reason, tend to promote some useful purpose; but compassion toward proper objects is the most beneficial of all the affections, and excites more lasting degrees of happiness, as it extends to greater numbers, and alleviates the infirmities and evils which are incident to human existence. Possessed of this amiable and Godlike disposition, Masons are shocked at misery under every form and appearance; When they behold an object pining under the miseries of a distressed body or mind, the healing accents which flow from the tongue mitigate the pain of the unhappy sufferer, and make even adversity, in its dismal state, look gay. When pity is excited, the Mason will assuage grief, and cheerfully relieve distress. If a brother be in want, every heart is moved; when he is hungry, we feed him; when he is naked, we clothe him; when he is in trouble, we fly to his relief. Thus we confirm the propriety of the title we bear; and convince the world at large that Brother, among Masons, is more than the name.'"

Having given these extracts, I feel bound to repeat, that we in England cannot, and do not accept those more high colored descriptions of Freemasonry which sometimes appear in foreign writers, because, as we believe, they are an exaggeration, and an hurtful exaggeration, of that simpler teaching of English Freemasonry, which, elevating itself above the turbid influences which seem some times to affect our foreign brethren, keeps firmly to its ancient landmarks, and objects equally to unproved novelties of practice and unsound theories of profession.

IV. There is a fourth theoretical objection made to Freemasonry, namely, that it is a secret society, and that secrecy is wrong alike by national law as on natural grounds. In fact, our assailants contend that secrecy is bad "per se," and alike improper and indefensible. Their argument, put into a syllogistic form, appears to be this- all secret societies are bad. Freemasonry is a secret society, therefore Freemasonry is bad. But are all secret societies bad? Here the whole point of the question is assumed and made universal. Now, it is not correct to say that all secret societies are "ipso facto" bad. All that can be fairly alleged is that all societies which use secrecy for an evil purpose are bad. No doubt all secret societies which are forbidden by the Legislature of any country are bad "per se" in the estimation of all good citizens, because contrary to that spirit of reverence for, and obedience to the laws of the land which is our boast ever in our own favored country, and ought to be characteristic always of a free people everywhere. It must be, indeed, a very special case, the fact alone of openly illegal and unrighteous tyranny, as well by the law of God as by the constitutions of men, that could ever afford the slightest justification for a secret society's continuance in opposition to the condemnation of the Legislature.

Indeed, I am very doubtful if such a state of things could ever exist which would justify the enduring of a secret society forbidden by a Government or by statute. For the Legislature has always a right to say "virtute officii," inherent and unimpeachable, we object to all secret societies whatever; and if the Legislature did actually say so, Freemasons, as good citizens and patriot subjects, would at once obey the law. But when has the Legislature said so with regard to Freemasons- at any rate, in Great Britain, The Legislature has, indeed, forbidden certain secret societies by name with avowed political or revolutionary ends, societies which use the cloak of secrecy to cover the designs of their untoward organization, or for the purpose of administering unlawful oaths- that is, oaths which are considered to be unlawful oaths by the statute or common laws of the realm. But the Legislature, while it has done so, has excepted Freemasonry "nominatim" from any such penalties or condemnation in the very Act which seeks to suppress such political associations, and I have always felt, as most of my brethren have felt, and as we all have a right to feel at this very hour, that our order has received not only toleration but sanction even in its secret character from the Legislature of our land.

That, as regards national laws, is surely defense sufficient for us, as no one can with any right pretend to believe that here in Great Britain our Masonic secrecy is in any way opposed to the general or municipal laws of our great English Fatherland. And how is it in respect of natural grounds? Is secrecy objectionable really and truly on natural grounds as between man and man. I know "Nemo" has said so lately in a controversy about some Roman Catholic views of Freemasonry in the "Times," but I do not see it, and cannot understand how it is so.

Do any of my readers?

How do this injustice and wrong arise 1 It is a very curious fact in the history of the world and of man, that so many of the old religions of the world were practically secret to the many, and that the most sacred mysteries were ever jealously guarded, and shrouded in mysterious secrecy and awe! To speak correctly, there is no natural wrong or ground as between man and man, except such as is founded on laws Divine or human.

If it might be contended that secrecy was bad "per se" as between man and man, it could only be, supposing that nothing had tainted the nature or marred the perfect condition of the open trust and actual relationship of man! But, as we know, no such perfect creation or condition exist here, or now, it is far too airy and rhapsodical a position to reach unto, for the objector to Masonic secrecy to invoke the "natural grounds," as between us and our fellow creatures. And even as regards man himself, secrecy in one sense may be said to be needful to man, a token ever of man's allotted frailty, since many things here are and ever must remain "secret" from our fellow-creatures; and it is alone an attribute of Divine power and omniscience that the secrets of man's heart and life are open to Him, though hidden from man even to the last.

I am aware of no other "natural grounds" on which secrecy is objectionable. Indeed, it is quite clear to me that, as between man and man, there is no law, on natural grounds, which renders secrecy wrong "per se;" and it is altogether a far-fetched and ill-advised notion of natural right and equity to lay down any such proposition!

So long as secret societies are not condemned by the legislature or laws of a country, there is nothing in them, that I can see, on any other ground to be improper or unrighteous. When forbidden by the legislature, they become wrong to all good citizens; and wherever even prohibition to Freemasonry still exists, I for one would not attend a lodge meeting in any portion of the world, where the local legislation forbade the assembling of Freemasons in lodge for Masonic purposes, on any grounds whatever.

But the attack on Freemasonry, as regards "secrecy," comes with a very bad grace from Roman Catholics; indeed, only exemplifies once more the great truth of the oft-used and well-known saying, "du sublime au ridicule il n'y 'a qu' un pas." Some one has said, and the saying is a good one in its way, that the Church of Home is the greatest secret society in the world!

And who is there that knows anything of the Jesuit order, with its secret vows, and "Monita Secreta" and hidden "formulae," and esoteric teaching; or of the "secrets" of the confessional, or of the secret vows and inner life of monasteries and nunneries; or of secret conclaves, and secret agencies!- who is there, I say, who has studied all these things, but must feel that secrecy is a great characteristic of the inward and outward organization of the Roman Catholic Church?

It is in vain, then, on any grounds of common sense, or

fair ratiocination, or even "natural grounds," for Roman Catholic authorities to denounce, anathematize, and excommunicate Freemasons, until they put a stop to their own secret societies and practices. It is, indeed, rather an act of no little hardihood in them to profess to find fault with the secret system of Freemasonry, while such secret societies and practices are openly avowed and permitted and commended under the very sanction oi the Pope. If ever there was a case where the Freemason could fairly say, in solemn words, to each intolerant adversary, and each excited accuser, "Physician, heal thyself," it is when, as recently, the Archbishop of Malines excommunicated all the Belgian Freemasons "en bloc" when Archbishop Manning condemned, inferentially, all Masonic organization whatever; when the "Westminster Gazette" declared that, as a secret society anathematized by Papal edicts, no Roman Catholic and no honest man can properly belong to our useful order; and when, above all, the humane and pious Pontiff himself, Pio Nino, in his allocution to the Brazilian Bishops, used language more vehement than polite, and more savory than sweet.

I think I have shown unanswerably, that neither on national grounds, or on natural grounds, or on religious grounds, can our Masonic secrecy be successfully impugned or condemned; and that I have done so, I trust that my readers will both now see and believe!

Though one of the commonest objections made against Freemasonry, it is one which has always appeared to me most weak and frivolous; as supposing for one moment, that Freemasons were to make their society an open society, (which, of course, they never can or will consent to do), what would our objectors gain? The principles on which Freemasonry is founded would still endure, namely, those of universality and philanthropic sympathy for all brethren of the dust! And as these are, after all, the main objects of inculpation, not any of the conditions by which Freemasonry has surrounded itself; whatever effect such a change might have on Freemasonry proper, it would in no way diminish or take away the continued existence of those great landmarks of Freemasonry, which stand out so boldly ever to the annoyance of many and the disapproval of more.

There is one other aspect of the case as regards the objection against secrecy which I must also consider before I pass on. It is sometimes said that if Freemasons had anything worth disclosing, they would not keep it secret, and that they must be ashamed of something or other, or they would not hide it from popular observation, and guard it as a mystery from the generality of mankind. I need hardly, I think, stop long now, to point out what a fallacy is contained in both these ill-considered assertions. Whether Freemasonry be right or wrong in throwing a veil of secrecy over its proceedings, and concealing its ceremonial usages from the public gaze and cognizance, is a matter I apprehend solely for Freemasons themselves to decide. But this one thing is certain, that because secrecy may be adopted on special grounds, and for a distinct end, it is not a case of "sequitur," either that that which is concealed is valueless, or that there is no useful end to be reached by the continuance of secrecy.

The very history of Christianity itself supplies the true answer to these somewhat popular objections, as there was a time when a veil of secrecy Was equally thrown, for especial purposes, over sacred rites and Scriptural teaching; but yet he would be a bold man who would contend either that that was worthless which was kept hidden from the profane, or that they were wrong who jealously guarded their spirituality from the prying, the perverse, and the persecutor. Freemasonry in its own inherent right, and with its own distinct views, professes still to say, as was said of old, when mysterious impressive ceremonies were duly performed, "procul Profani," and who shall venture to say in so speaking and in so acting, Freemasonry is not entirely "dans son droit!" I, for one most certainly think, and unhesitatingly say, that the secrecy of Freemasonry is right and proper from whatever point of view you look at it; and is a characteristic of our order, which, while it marks clearly before all men one great condition of Freemasonry, is one for which numerous arguments may be adduced to prove its value, its importance, and its need. For unlike every other society, I believe, in the world, the one answer of Freemasonry to all applicants for light and knowledge, ever has been and still is, and ever will be, the same. Freemasonry asks no one to become a Freemason. Freemasons never "tout" for candidates, to use a common expression. Freemasons never advertise the benefits of Freemasonry, merely to increase its numbers; and after a long experience, I can fairly say this today, and all my brethren will support my assertion, that it is one of die most observed standing rules and regulations of Freemasonry never to seek to procure a neophyte by invitation or persuasion of any kind whatever.

But all worthy men of competent age, sound morals, respectable citizens, and worthy members of society, we are glad to accept into our brotherhood, if only they can receive a proper introduction and a satisfactory voucher. Therefore, our answer as Freemasons still is, and will ever be, to an inquisitive world which complains of our secrecy, we maintain it, and shall maintain it for good and sufficient causes. And though in saying this I somewhat anticipate subsequent remarks, I think it well to place it before you now. If any persons feel that their sentiments and sympathies are akin to those which are claimed and owned by Freemasons, let them endeavor to obtain admission into our order, which though still surrounded by the conditions of solemn secrecy and mystic symbolism has yet enrolled under its goodly banners some of the best and most enlightened of our race, who have not been ashamed to join its fellowship and obey its laws.

The objection to Freemasonry, then, on the ground of secrecy is, generally, as I hope I have shewn you, a complete bugbear, made use of by the credulous, the perverse, or the ignorant, or the fanatic, to hinder as they idly hope, the advance of an Institution which, wherever it is firmly planted and rightly appreciated, becomes an untiring advocate for freedom of thought, and the rights of conscience, for toleration and charity, for the elevating and ennobling development of intellectual culture, brotherly goodwill, and consistent morality. It has flourished in past times, it will continue to flourish, I believe to day, despite the feeble platitudes of illogical adversaries; and turning neither to the right nor to the left, it marches on its way, true to its own principles, and faithful to its appointed mission.

I have hitherto been considering the objection of secrecy almost entirely objectively, that is in its theoretical aspect purely. I propose now to treat it subjectively as regards our Masonic body itself We have, as Freemasons, many reasons for secrecy.

It has been well said by a brother in an Australian Masonic publication that "many are prejudiced against our order, because ours is a 'secret society.' Our secrecy too frequently has been the innocent cause of the persecutions and molestations to which our brethren have been subjected at the hands of 'the popular world' Bigotry or hyperorthodoxy has often shown itself 'splenetic and rash' against our Fraternity. Even in our day, in a troubled sea of passion tossed, there are Cowans found, who frown and storm at us, because of 'our secrecy.' But, is 'secrecy' a great evil? Is taciturnity a virtue or a vice? 'Speech is silver; silence is golden,' says the adage. 'Beden Kommt von Natur, Schweigen von Veratunde,' say the inhabitants of 'Fatherland.' (Talking comes by nature, silence by understanding.) 'Odi, vedi, e taci'- (Hear, see, and say nothing)- is the truly Masonic saying of the Italians. If the scoffers at our Masonic silence be professing theologians, then let them learn a lesson on silence from the Old Book. The Hon. Robert Boyle says- 'There is such fullness in that book that oftentimes it says much by saying nothing; and not only its expressions but its silences are teaching; like the dial, on which the shadow, as well as the light, gives us information.' 'Tie your tongue,' said a great and good man, 'lest it be wanton and luxuriate: keep it within the banks; a rapidly flowing river soon collects mud.' Are our fault-finders students of the Great Book of Nature? Then does not every object of creation furnish hints for their contemplation? Does not even the most minute and mean in Nature's works teach some important truth? Let them rise on contemplation's wings and gaze on the silence which reigns around. Look- that nightly star shines in silence; every day turns the axle of the earth in silence; the glorious orb of light works mighty things in silence; look at our motionless torrents- our silent cataracts; look even at those spires, whose 'silent finger points to heaven,' and is not silence 'the perfectest herald of joy' to a contemplative mind? But me- thinks, the anti-Masonic still sneer at our Masonic silence and secrecy. Alas, hopelessly...

> 'Fixed and contemplative their looks
> Still turning over Nature's books'

...they have formed the determination not to see the wisdom or the dignity of our Masonic 'silent might!' Moreover, does the Great Architect Himself not set the glorious example of silence before us, when He conceals from mankind the secrets of His Providence. Can any of our anti-Masonic friends penetrate into the arcana of heaven? Can they foretell today what tomorrow may bring forth? And is not silence of the utmost importance in the different transactions of life?"

"It is true that unprincipled men may abuse their secrecy, as some have done, and their system, instead of being a system of 'superior light and knowledge' may become a system of 'atrocity and crime.' But the religious system of Freemasony is not to be likened to the irreligious system of the mistaken or perverse. And consequently our religious Masonic silence is not that dreadful bell which should fright our censors from their propriety. What!- do our detractors wish us to be noisy and turbulent disputants? Are we to make night and day hideous by controversial howls and disputatious explosions? The greatest talkers are always the least doers. Spare to speak and spare to speed. Noble examples there are, then, from whom we may learn the wisdom, the power, and the dignity of secrecy. Consequently, in spite of the maligning of our anti-Masonic revilers, contemplate the silent magnanimity of every 'worthy Mason' who with a well-constituted mind silently squares his life upon the principles of moral truth and justice, and though the hand of death be upon him, betrays not his sacred trust, but with unshaken fidelity 'locks up the secrets in his heart.' Then is not our secrecy- our wisdom, our might, our dignity? And does not our silence 'answer much.'"

> "'True prayer is not the noisy sound
> That clamorous lips repeat,
> But the deep silence of a soul
> That clasps Jehovah's feet.'

It has been most truly also observed by one of the oldest and ablest of our Masonic papers in the United States, that the secrecy of our order is defensible on other grounds. In all the transactions of life, between man and man, there are numerous occasions when it is neither necessary nor prudent that the world should be admitted to the counsels of the parties. No private association of individuals conducts its meetings with open doors, and public bodies have reserved to themselves the right of holding secret sessions whenever, in their own opinion, the interests of the country require a concealment of their deliberations. Merchants do not expose their books to the free inspection of the community; lawyers do not detail at the corners of the streets the confidential communications of their clients; nor do physicians make the private disclosures of their patients the topic of their ordinary conversation. Juries determine in impenetrable privacy on the lives, the fortunes, and the reputations of their fellow-citizens; and legislative bodies often discuss the most important questions that involve the policy of the nation in the sacred security of secret session. Why, then, from Masonry should this necessary safeguard he withheld? Why should that practice, which in all other Institutions is considered right and proper, he only deemed improper when pursued by Masons? And why, of all men, should we alone be disfranchised of the universal privilege to select our own confidants, and to conduct our own business in the way and manner which, without injury to others, we deem most beneficial to ourselves? If by the charge of secrecy our opponents would accuse us of having invented and preserved certain modes of recognition confined to ourselves, and by which one Mason may know another in the dark as well as the light, while we willingly and proudly admit the accusation, we boldly deny the criminality of the practice. If in a camp surrounded by enemies it has always been deemed advisable to establish countersigns and watchwords, whereby the weary sentinel may be enabled to distinguish the friendly visit of a comrade from the hostile incursions of a foe, by a parity of reasoning every other association has an equal right to secure its privacy and confine its advantages, whatever they may be, within its own bosom, by the adoption of any system which will sufficiently distinguish those who are its members from those who are not. When a University grants a diploma, it seeks to give to each alumnus a test of membership and of recognition."

"The mode of recognition, or what is the same thing, the proof of membership furnished by Masonry to its disciples, differs in no respect from this, except that it is far more perfect. The diploma which our institution bestows upon its disciples is far more enduring than a roll of parchment- time can never efface the imperishable characters inscribed upon it- neither moth nor rust can corrupt it, nor thieves break through and steal it. As fair and legible after years of possession, as it was in the day of its reception, the zealous and attentive Mason carries it with him wherever he moves, and is ready at all times, and in all places to prove by its unmistakable authority his claim to the kindness and protection of his brethren. The secrecy of our mode of recognition is our safeguard. It furnishes each member of the Craft and the whole Fraternity with a security against imposition, and by readily and certainly supplying a means of detection, it prevents the unprincipled and dishonest from falsely assuming the appearance of virtuous poverty, and thus preserves for the treasury of the society its charitable funds to be more appropriately bestowed upon the destitute brother, the distressed widow and the helpless orphans. As the watchword would cease to be a protection to the sleeping camp, if it were publicly announced at the head of the army, instead of being confined by a wise precaution to the guard on duty, so the secret mode of recognition among Masons, if promulgated to the world, would no longer enable us to detect imposition, or to aid true brethren. In this there can be no crime, for we thus invade no man's right, but only more securely protect our own. But it is said that Freemasons have certain traditions, and practice certain ceremonies, which we religiously preserve from the knowledge of all but the initiated. But unless it would be proved that these traditions were corrupting, or those ceremonies licentious, we know not on what basis a charge of criminality could rest. Yet more. Could it even be alleged that the former were imaginary, and the latter ludicrous, they would still be simply harmless. But when we know that with the one there is connected a vast fund of historical truth, and legendary lore, and that the other symbolically communicates lessons profoundly moral and religious, we best secure their integrity and purity. Were these secrets to be indiscriminately dispersed, they would soon lose their value- becoming familiar, they would cease to be important, and that which was no man's peculiar property would find not one to protect it from corruption, or to preserve it from oblivion. If there be any suspicion that there are mysteries which are carefully covered with the veil of secrecy, we would state, that our doors, though closed to the unworthy, are ever open to the knocks of the deserving. To the good man and true, there need be no mysteries in Masonry with which he is unacquainted. If he be offended that he does not share our confidence, we say to him, approach the vestibule of our Temple, show on your part a willingness to mingle in our devotions, and we will gladly embrace you as a fellow worship per at our altar- to you we will readily impart what we have received, and with you, will investigate all the doctrines, ceremonies and symbols, which constitute the esoteric work of

Freemasonry."

"But if from indifference to truth, or an indisposition to investigate, you are unwilling to seek this entrance within our walls, then we demand of you, in all fairness and candor, that you will at least cease to reproach or censure us for the exclusive possession of secrets, in the ownership of which you yourself have refused to participate."

I think that I need add nothing more under this head, as the words: I have just quoted, put the case for Freemasons as regards the value of secrecy to them, as justly and clearly as possible. I have now exhausted the objections to Freemasonry in the abstract- that is to say, those which appear to me to deserve any attention or consideration, for, as I before ventured to observe, some objections, of both old and of quite modern times, even so late as this very year of grace and light, are so inane and so puerile in themselves that they certainly do not merit, as they certainly will not receive, your attention, kindly readers, or mine. I, however, now propose to take up the allegations made against Freemasonry in the concrete.

I. The first one which I shall seek to deal with under this second great division, or head, is one in truth very serious in itself, and which, when put forward religiously and "bona fide," has a right to claim to be carefully considered and respectfully dealt with by Freemasons, for all conscientious scruples and all fair antagonism, however outspoken, ought always to be met, in my humble opinion, by a spirit of friendly seriousness and calm reasoning. Freemasons, from their unceasing teaching of courtesy to all, of forbearance with all, never think lightly of, or affect to disregard or disdain either the scruples of an honest inquirer or the forcible animadversions of an honorable opponent; and the allegation thus made against Freemasonry, shortly stated, is, the ignoring of Christianity and of the Christian Church, a deliberate negation of Christianity altogether, the offering up of prayer to

A DEFENSE OF FREEMASONRY

Almighty God in which professing Christians join, with- out the name of a Savior or a Mediator being recognized and made use of.

Hence it is averred that no sincere Christian can rightly belong to a society which thus denies and neglects one of the great foundation truths of Christianity and the Church. Now this is an objection frequently raised by members of all denominations, not by one alone, and meet it, therefore, we must. As a fact it is true and undeniable, and how, then, as Freemasons, do we propose to explain it or justify it? No doubt, as a general rule, for all Christians since the promulgation of Christianity and the setting up of the Church, all prayers offered up to our Heavenly Father- with two exceptions- are so offered in the name and through the mediation of the common Savior of mankind. But one prayer has ever also been used by all Christians, which is simply a petition to a common Father in Heaven, and if, to Christians, as they believe, a reconciled and covenant Father in Christ, yet still the Father of mankind, whether to Christians or Hebrew or heathen, the Great Architect of the World alike for good and bad.

Since 1813 Freemasonry in England has confined itself purely to that divine model of prayer, the Lord's Prayer, for all our religious services and invocations, leaving out entirely any question of Christian dogma or teaching, and thus all our Masonic prayers have become, if I may so say, "Universal" alike in substance and in design.

There have been Christian prayers in use in English Freemasonry, especially during the latter part of the last century. Christian prayers are still used, I believe, both in Scotland and Ireland, but their use has not mitigated the objections against Freemasonry, which go deeper, and extend, in fact, to the whole system of our Brotherhood.

And the reason of this "Universalism" is, I repeat, obvious. If Freemasonry, rightly or wrongly, proposes to include in its ample fold- as it undoubtedly does propose to include alike Christian and Hebrew; and even for Hindus and Mohammedans there Would be but little hope, for instance, of any fraternal union or concord, if in our lodges the prayers we use for peace and piety's sake were to become the cause of contention, the ground of complaint, even for Non-christian members.

The Christian brethren may indeed say, (as has been contended), that the Hebrew brethren, for instance, ought to accept the Christian prayers; but the Hebrew brethren would admit of no such obligation lying upon them; and as Freemasonry has nothing to do with Proselytism, and purports to be a society universal in its scope and object, all its prayers must be necessarily universal also. Some one has suggested that, in order to meet this difficulty, lodges should be formed for religionists of different denominations alone, but that would be only "daubing the wall with untempered mortar;" and if this "religious difficulty" was partially removed here today by such a system, it would only crop up more seriously and acrimoniously elsewhere tomorrow.

Indeed, such a plan could but be, humanly speaking, the prelude to endless controversial strife, and the foundation assuredly of never-ending "odium theologicum et lathomicum."

For in so acting Freemasonry would at once recognize these religious differences, which abound among Christians and the world at large, which at present it utterly ignores, and therefore, whether for good or for evil, our English Grand Lodge has put forth an universal program, and the Lord's Prayer has, both theoretically and practically, become the simple form and foundation of all Masonic prayers, being one which all can join in unquestioningly, and being one which all can equally accept in some sense and in some way. It is possible, I do not conceal from myself, nor from those for whom I now write, that the attitude of Freemasonry, in this respect, debars many worthy men from joining our order, but in my humble opinion, Freemasonry is right in thus endeavoring on its own universal principles, to associate in a common expression of prayer to a common Maker and Master, those who might otherwise have remained at an immeasurable distance from each other.

To some minds this position of Freemasonry is an insuperable objection alike to its constitution and its proceedings, but as I previously endeavored to point out, our universal profession is the great keystone of the true Masonic Arch, and the fundamental teaching of all our formularies, and once loosen the one, or seek to remove the other, the Arch itself must give way necessarily, must crumble into pieces, and leave us nothing but shattered pillars and mournful "debris."

For by thus sapping the foundation of the universal teaching of our fraternity, you erase at once that great and world-wide charter of liberty of thought and toleration of teaching, which renders Freemasonry a meeting place and a resting place for all, who, accepting a Common Father, are glad to be able to join together in works of sympathy, or efforts of benevolence, in social intercourse, and in the religious expression of active and consistent morality. And if it be said that by our very constitution some of our members may not accept the Divine laws of morality and brotherly love, then we must appeal to those immutable laws of self-control, self-moderation, and self-elevation, of honesty, and temperance, of honor and truthfulness, of good living, and of solemn duty, which are written in the heart, and accepted by the conscience of us all!

Freemasonry in my humble opinion, has at any rate, the clear right, to say this, You may condemn my principles of action and adhesion, but at any rate, shew me what yours are worth as regards practical proof. There are 250 millions of Christians in the world or thereabouts, and the remaining two-thirds of our fellow-creatures are Non-Christian. Are we to utterly discard them, and ignore them, in the great struggle of life, and in any works of kindness and benevolence? Even if all Christians were at one it would be something, but Christians unfortunately are anathematizing or antagonizing one another with a bitterness and a virulence which tend more than anything else to hinder the spread of the civilizing and elevating and healing influence of the Christian Church, and are an undissembled source of malignant joy to the infidel and the scorner.

Why then have you a right to find fault with a society, which if on lower grounds, has yet succeeded to some extent at any rate, in its aim and effect, and does actually at this time include within one body, not only Christians of various denominations, but even Hebrews, Hindus, Mohammedans, and Parsees?

And in truth the Christian reply to this question is a very difficult one to make. I have never seen a good reply to it, unless indeed, that one which is practically the same in all denominations be made use of, "Extra ecclesiam nulla salus."

But, as I said at the outset, I do not deny for one moment, that, an earnest religionist may find the difficulty insuperable, and may think himself bound by his professions of Christianity to disapprove of, and to decline to take part in the proceedings of a society which thus to his mind ignores what he considers to be a fundamental truth and obligation of Christianity. As a Freemason I can only leave the objection to itself. I see no force or validity in it whatever, though it will probably always be raised in many pious minds, and by many excellent men. Yet as Freemasonry cannot alter what is the very essence of its constitution, without jeopardizing the existence of the entire goodly and stately building, as Freemasons cannot sweep away the universality of their principles, in deference to hostile animadversions, our Order must continue to fall under the ban of some, the persecution of others, the excommunication even of the intolerant and the unreasoning. Freemasonry despite many attacks, and boldly facing many enemies, is happily enabled nevertheless to march on its way, in all the calmness of conscious strength and peaceful unity, unfurling its broad banner of toleration and brotherhood over its more than sacred "phalanx" of loyal, and upright, and honorable, and devoted citizens, our myriads of "good men and true", faithful comrades in Masonry. Under this head of objection comes in necessarily also the charge of "Indifferentism," one not uncommonly made against Freemasonry. Let us listen for a moment to the serious accusations of the "Church Herald," under this head.

"But we have further objections, and they are these: Freemasonry is notoriously founded on a basis of religious indifference. No matter what a man's religion is, he may become 'a member of the Craft.' Now, faith, as the necessity of holding certain tenets and of believing certain dogmas, is of the essence of Christianity, so the very antithesis of this true and good principle- a stolid and steady indifference to all religious doctrine, the hearty welcome and formal reception of True and False alike into the bosom of Freemasonry is to that system at once the condition and cause of its existence. Hence it is perfectly idle of our correspondent to write about 'immense sums known to be annually expended among Masons in private charity.' Charity does not and cannot exist among Masons- philanthropy may (and possibly does), but philanthropy and charity have different roots, different stems, and by consequence, different fruits. A leading English Mason allowed us to take down the following from his lips, only last week: 'If to myself, as a Freemason, two persons in equally distressed circumstances came for temporal relief, the one being a Christian, and the other a Brahmin; and the Brahmin signified that he belonged to our fraternity, and the Christian did not, I should be bound to relieve the Brahmin in preference to the Christian. In that rests the beauty and value of our benevolence and true charity.' One is Pagan and Heathen: the other is Christian. No matter then, how benevolent its intentions and deeds may be (if benevolent they are), Freemasonry is absolutely and altogether incompatible with Christianity. Its essential and leading principle (as an outsider can see, and as no Mason can deny), is Indifferentism. 'It does not matter one iota of what religion you are. One is as good as another- or as bad as another- if people like to put the question in that form. Mahommedanism to a Mason is as good as Christianity, and Christianity as Buddhism. We have Mahommedan Masons, Protestant Masons, Buddhist Masons, and Deistical Masons. It is all one with us. Each is welcomed. They are all fish which come to the wide-meshed net of Freemasonry.' And this, we need not say, is naked Indifferentism. Now speculative Indifferentism leads directly to Pantheism. A Mason and a Christian, therefore, if each be true to his Creed, can no more mix than fire and water. Here in England some of the lodges may be harmless as regards action; but none can be untouched or untainted by the false principle already set forth, which is at the root of the subject. Masonry substitutes humanitarianism for Christianity, using Christians to cover its designs and aid its purposes. To belong to any lodge, therefore, a man must practically forswear the Church and deny Christ; or (we are charitable in our alternative), act in invincible ignorance of the leading and avowed principles of the Craft."

Such is the allegation of "Indifferentism" made against us by our latest assailant, which I now propose to consider. I will dismiss at once the "leading English Mason," as whoever he may be, his utterances are alike utterly nonsensical and unreliable- assertions perfectly childish and ridiculous- parodies on the recognized teaching of our Order. Indeed, I am inclined to fancy, that the leading English Mason is a mythical personage altogether, an ingenuous Bro. "Harris" raised up for the nonce, to come to the aid of the "Church Herald" on the "amicus curiae" principle.

As I have said before, Freemasonry is certainly a resting place, a rallying point, for all religious denominations, and in that sense, though not with any real indifferentism, Freemasonry ignores all controversial questions, and all the severances of conflicting creeds. But Freemasonry nowhere substitutes "humanitarianism" for Christianity, inasmuch as Freemasonry does not profess, as I before pointed out, to be a "Religio" to any.

All it really does is, accepting the grand idea of one brotherhood, it seeks to carry that idea into action by putting on one side altogether the religious differences and divisions of men, and forming them into one great and comprehensive sodality, of good-will and sympathy and mutual regard.

Such writers as the one whose "outcome" I am now considering, of course despise such a notion as savoring of "indifferentism," if not of something much worse.

Indeed, the scribe in the "Church Herald," though clearly out of his depth altogether, goes on to say "that speculative indifference leads to Pantheism," that "a Mason and a Christian, if each be true to his creed, can no more mix than fire and water," and "that to belong to any lodge, a man must practically forsake the Church and deny Christ." Is it not sad to realize to what length fanaticism will lead some, and a hopeless incapacity of reasoning others?

Here is a writer, professedly a Christian man, positively unchristianizing thousands of his fellow-men, simply because they are Freemasons, forgetting that men of the most undoubted Christian piety, and most faithful members of the Church, have gladly joined, and still belong to our maligned order. What can anyone reply to an opponent who is so uncharitable or so perversely obtuse? To him, the mere fact of Christians and Non-christians meeting for benevolent purposes is a subject of the deepest distress, as if in some mysterious way, Freemasonry was a standing injury, or menace, or danger to the true Church and the Christian faith.

Now, what I have always contended for is, that Freemasonry being external to the Church, the Church has nothing to do with its principles, its professions, or its practices, save in respect of its own members. The Church might as well anathematize savings banks, or science, (as has been the case,) or any provident or friendly institution.

The days of pilgrimages have returned, it is said, are we to witness the revival of anathemas and interdicts? To this point all seems tending just now in many quarters.

The Church of Home excommunicates the Freemasons, practically, everywhere. There is, as Mr. Cuffe contended, a standing interdict against them in her communion, so much so, that when a Roman Catholic becomes a Freemason, he ceases to be a Roman Catholic altogether.

And the Ritualists, weak imitators of Borne, are actually trying to do the same thing, and to say the same thing, though at present their efforts are very puny and very puerile.

Yet, despite it all, and despite them all, Roman and Ritualist, and Reformed Presbyterian alike, the old Craft is wafted on by a favoring breeze, and leaves its truly Christian accusers to that "odium theologicum" they so much love to join in, and those mournful controversies which have so greatly impeded Christianity, and so much disgraced mankind.

A writer in the "American Freemason" has recently put the matter of Masonic toleration so well, that I have considered it advisable to close this section of my reply and defense with his thoughtful and judicious words. "Freemasonry upholds and preserves the inalienable right of every man, to think, speak, and act for himself on those topics which we hold to be the personal attributes of each individual, subject only to the monitions of his own conscience, and the laws of the Supreme Architect. As a body of men, embracing every rank and condition of respectable society, they never think of saying or doing anything that may give offense to a neighbor's way of thinking, religiously or politically. Each one, reserving the right of private judgment, freely accords the same privilege to his neighbor, and lightning is scarcely more prompt than would be the official call to order should any one attempt to introduce a religious or political topic of discussion in a lodge. Masonry is simply a moral institution, opening its doors to good men of every sect and opinion, and while it requires no profession of faith beyond those great underlying principles which all men who have any religious inspiration at all agree with; it asks no man his mode of faith, but leaves that where it belongs-between the individual conscience and the Supreme Being. And to these conditions, we repeat again, because we desire it to be specially impressed on the mind of the reader, the great body of the craft are entirely faithful. Masonry has no propaganda of the faith; Masons never have and never can learn, from what is taught them in the lodge, any thing by which they may be incited to choose one means of serving the Deity rather than another; on the contrary, every instruction given, every charge and lecture tends to demonstrate the desire of the institution that, while every man should be moral, and even religious, he must choose for himself the particular path he will follow, and seek outside the pale of Masonry the counsel and instruction he may deem necessary in making his choice. If the reader will think for a moment he will see how utterly impossible it would be for the fraternity to occupy any other ground; how insuperable and how destructive of all harmony it would be if there were the slightest wavering to the right hand or to the left from the straight and narrow road marked out for us, and which, with undeviating accuracy, leads us apart and away from every possible difference of opinion on theological subjects. In our ranks are represented every shade of religious opinion and difference, and it necessarily follows that any appreciable leaning toward one more than another would be the signal for an eternal war that would rend the association to its very base, and make all the wondrous prosperity we are now enjoying but the foil of a disaster such as few men have dreamed of."

And here I leave the matter, despite the anathema of the fanatic and the intolerant, as I am quite ready on all occasions to uphold the truly religious position of Freemasonry in this respect.

II. Another objection has been made of old, and repeated in our own time quite recently, that Freemasonry forms a bond of spurious union among men, inasmuch as it is outside the distinct teaching of the Church and of the Gospel.

This view has also been propounded in the "Church Herald," as well as by Mr. Kerr, of Greenock, with more zeal than discretion, in the following words:

"For ourselves, not being Freemasons, we know nothing whatever about the system except what every outsider may know. The following fact, however, is evident to all outsiders, that Freemasonry is a system that sets up in the world an unity utterly distinct from, and wholly independent of, if not directly antagonistic to, the Church or Family of Jesus Christ. The sacred bond of baptism, the principle of Christian fellowship, is ignored, and a new and unknown principle (but a very real and energizing one) is adopted, which is common at once to lax Christians and heathens. As a practical example of what we mean, we may just put on record the following remarks, made in France by Abd-el-Kaier, a Mason but a heathen: 'In my opinion every man who does not profess Freemasonry (which I consider to be the first institution in the world) is an incomplete man.' At a banquet of Masons of Gloucestershire and Worcestershire a certain Dr. Bowles, an English clergyman, commenting on the Pope's well-known Allocution against Freemasonry, in quoting the above with approbation, remarked: 'It seems to me that Abd-el-Kader, Infidel though he be, is a far better Christian than the Pope.' Thus Dr. Bowles avowedly prefers, and glories in preferring, the liberty of the Infidel to the exclusiveness of Christianity- in other words, Humanitarianism to the Faith, by and through the principle (whatever it be) of Freemasonry. This is our chief and great objection to it, and to every believer in the Incarnation it ought to be sufficient to warn him from having anything whatsoever to do with such an institution. On this point an outsider is perfectly competent to express an opinion."

It is quite clear to me that the writer of the above injudicious and vehement remarks cannot give a calm consideration either to the facts of the case or to the avowed object of Freemasonry. Freemasons nowhere propose or profess to set up an unity utterly distinct from, and wholly independent of, if not entirely antagonistic to, the Church and family of our Redeemer.

If the position of this assailant is good, no possible association is allowable here of Christians and of Non-christians.

Unless all accept Christian principles, and are guided by Christian "counsels," no union is possible and no combination allowable. All that Freemasonry seeks to do, then, believing this theory to be unsound, untrue, and really un-Christian, is to offer a meeting-place for persons of all denominations, in no spirit however of distinction or independence or antagonism to the Church. For independently of the fact that there is no unity whatever in the Church universal at present, therefore no antagonism can exist to her; it is practically a supposed opposition, therefore, which the writer has fancied here to some particular Church, be it that of Home, or England.

But, as I have often said, Freemasonry knows nothing of such antagonisms, and in that one sense, but only in that one sense, can it be said to be independent of the Christian Church. But it is only independent of the Church, not from any question of religious difference or hostility, but simply from its own position. Freemasonry enters into no question as to the dogmas of the Church, or the constitution of the Church, or the membership of the Church. All these things, good and right in their own province, have nothing to do with Freemasonry, and in no sense whatever does Freemasonry ever seek to come into collision with the Church, or claim anything like corresponding privileges and obligations, or a coordinate jurisdiction and sphere. Freemasonry has its own work, its own mission, and its own pathway to pursue, and, while it is friendly to all religious bodies, it is inimical and antagonistic to none.

With regard to the censure passed by this hasty writer on our good old brother, Dr. Bowles, all I understand him to say is, that the unrighteous condemnation by the Pope of Rome of Freemasonry, unheard, unaccused "ex mero motu," is so palpably unjust and so sadly un-Christian, that our Bro. Abd-el-Kader, Mahommedan though he was, had more truly entered into the tolerant spirit of the Christian religion, than the authorities who published so untrue, unrighteous, and offensive a decree against a peaceful and unoffensive body of men- those loyal subjects and those patriotic citizens who compose the Masonic body.

But when this same writer goes on to say and to declare "that the Church of Borne has again and again formally condemned Freemasonry, and we are among those who hold that such a condemnation is right, true, and timely; authority in the Roman Church has spoken, and spoken plainly; and, if we English Churchmen would seek and pray for union, we must not act in opposition to known principles, or ignore patent facts when re-union is being sought for," one can only express the deepest regret that any person on such idle grounds can accept the "ex parte" judgment of the Church of Borne on such a question without hesitation or doubt, and yet profess himself to be a loyal member of the Church of England. The Church of Borne has condemned Freemasonry over and over again on grounds peculiar to that anathematizing denomination, but I have yet to learn that a benevolent and beneficent society, whose works are patent to the whole world as are our works of charity and pious good will, is to be excommunicated simply because it seems good to an infallible Pontiff, so to speak, and because, without rhyme or reason, "Roma locuta est, causa finita est." Indeed, the Church of Borne most fully verifies, in her past and present position, versus Freemasonry, the great moralist's memorable adage, "Prejudice is a judgment formed beforehand without examination."

And it is most sad to notice in many of our young Anglican Ritualists today, that servile tendency to ape the worst follies and to copy the most grotesque extravagances of the Church of Borne. Now, it has always appeared to me that anything more injudicious than the course the Church of Borne has thought well to pursue as regards Freemasonry, and which some other religious bodies like the Ritualistic portion of the Anglican Church, and the Scottish Reformed Presbyterian Synods, and even some American Baptists, are similarly pursuing at the present time, never was suggested or adopted by any religious persuasion.

And when many talk so glibly of a "spurious bond of union," they only mean a "bond of union" outside their own peculiar Church, forgetting that Masonry is in one sense entirely independent of the organization of the Church, in consequence of its great principle of Universality, which is the dominant feature undoubtedly of Free-masonry, as we have it now. But the question also comes in necessarily here, "Is Freemasonry right or wrong on this actual point?"

On the avowed principles of Freemasonry, Freemasonry is undoubtedly right, as the objections of Mr. Kerr, a recent Presbyterian assailant, put into other words, are simply these under this head: "As Freemasonry does not think well to take the Reformed Presbyterian Synods' view of things, I boldly say that it is outside the Church, and forms a spurious bond of union." But how or why?

It is true that such bond of union is not formed on the principles of the Reformed Presbyterian Synod, nor, indeed, on those of any religious denomination, and therefore I can quite understand, as I once before said, how that the earnest religionist may not approve of the Masonic constitution or position in this respect. But one further question. What is a spurious bond of union?

Now, in answer to these queries, what Mr. Kerr and others deem a spurious bond of union, no doubt is an union founded on principles which are not fully Christian, according to his or their views. But how does Freemasonry form a "spurious bond of union," in inviting all men to aid in works of love, by greeting all who join a brotherhood for that purpose?

It may not be a bond of union we think the best, it may not be the bond of union which best accords with our own orthodox views, but is it opposed in any way to God's Word, or the true happiness of the world?

On the contrary, has not the Masonic bond of union- call it spurious if you will, anti-Christian if you like- done much in many portions of the globe for the peaceful progress and social welfare of mankind? Freemasonry, as I have often previously observed, sets up no spurious bond of union in opposition to any religious body, is in no way in antagonism to, or rivalry in respect of religious denominations, and simply asks to be left alone, and to pursue its own simple and tranquil and humanizing course, in all of sympathy and good will to all religious denominations, and to its fellow men.

But I know all earnest Christians do not and will not see the matter as I do, though it seems to be both easy, straightforward, and simple to myself. On the contrary, good men like Dr. Armstrong the Bishop of Giahamstown, and "Father Faber," and Mr. Kerr, and many members of religious bodies, have found fault with Freemasonry simply because it is external to the influences, and creeds, and organization of the Church, or to the denomination to which they respectively belonged.

A DEFENSE OF FREEMASONRY

I am, however, happy to be able to record here, that numbers of earnest Christians, both in England and the United States, several bishops of the American Episcopal Church, have found no difficulty whatever in accepting the "status" of Freemasonry, and; have never considered it in any way antagonistic to religion or to the Church. It appears to me that Freemasonry may claim for itself this merit, that, by its bond of union (call it what you like), it has succeeded in lifting itself and its members above the strife of tongues and the logomachy of intolerance.

Instead of finding fault with Freemasonry in this respect, we should rejoice to think that it has been given to us as Freemasons to point out to the world, that men can be united and knitted together by the links of an universal brotherhood, firmly, peacefully, lovingly, and securely.

And if some may still object that we do not join ourselves together as Christian brethren on Christian principles, we can only reply that, taking things as we find them, we make the best use of the present position of society and of the world; and that while others are contending here, and excommunicating there, we, heedless of censure, and regardless of obloquy, pursue the "even tenor" of our peaceful way, looking on from the very divisions and separations of today, to the great Brotherhood of men, the "federation of the world," one day, in God's own good time to be.

Imperfect as our organization may be in itself and in its principles, it is ever distinguished by sincerity, kindly feeling, forbearance, and sympathy for others; and it represents, I believe, in its universal form and adaptation, the unceasing want of humanity, the great living yearning of this human heart of ours for unity and Brotherhood and for love of one another.

Like all purely earthly institutions, and all incomplete arrangements in this life, it may be destined in the fullness of time, as an entire organization, to give way or to make way for one more perfect and more enduring.

But as Freemasonry has clearly its place and work and mission in the world, and keeping before us always how it has subserved and promulgated fraternal charity, mitigated suffering, and advanced the moral and the best interests of mankind, we may rejoice to remember that in successive ages of human selfishness and separation, Free- masonry, despite its inevitable earthly weaknesses and shortcomings, its imperfections, and the many spots on its "feasts of charity," has set an example here, which all may equally advance and imitate- of brotherly union, kindness, concord, and good will. "Spurious" though its bond of union may be unrightly termed, by the narrow or the captious, it has conciliated firm friendships amid men of differing climes, religions, and language, and has in this country of late years been remarkably prominent, in inducing its members to many combined exertions for the promotion of true charity and the extension of education, succor, and relief.

In this great world of ours, with its teeming multitudes, and the mighty contest ever waging between good and evil, and happiness and sorrow, surrounded as we are ever here by innumerable forms of suffering and wretchedness of every kind, the Church, one should "prima facie" be disposed to imagine, might gladly welcome the aid, and encourage the efforts of Freemasonry. If it be true that we do not agree on all points, we do, nevertheless, concur in this, that we are all anxious to diminish and mitigate as far as we can the presence of earthly calamity, and the burdens of human woe.

That surely is a warfare which all may wage, a struggle in which all may take part, a toil in which all may share; and I feel certain myself, that Christian bodies, instead of assailing, instead of denouncing Freemasons, would do much better if they sought to meet Freemasons half way, and utilized their unceasing endeavors, and encouraged their unwearied labors for the relief of distress, for the sustentation of old age, the education of the orphan, and the care of the widow! Here, surely, is a nobler sphere both of duty and devotion than hateful controversies or cruel animosities- here is an arena in which we all may strive honorably who can most distinguish ourselves, who can most excel- here is a school in which all scholars may learn the truest discipline of life in love and sympathy for our fellow creatures. And from these good laborers of love and philanthropy, I make bold to add, when the great army is at last numbered of faithful workers, and comrades, and soldiers, when the last great roll call is gone through, that the Grand Master of us all will summon his most devoted craftsmen here into His own beatific mansions of light, and goodness, and bliss.

III: I now come to the third practical objection, that Freemasonry is a secret political society, with irreligious and revolutionary and destructive principles; socialistic even in its tenets, and dangerous in its results alike to civil order and national interests!

Such seems to be the last official Roman Catholic view of the subject, as we have been recently warned, by special allocutions of the Roman Catholic Archbishop of Malines, by Archbishop Manning, though in a subdued strain; by the "Westminster Gazette," a Roman Catholic journal, published in England; by several excited Roman Catholic bishops; and even by the venerable Pio Nono himself.

And, moreover, a Ritualistic Anglican paper, the "Church Herald" (the zeal of perverts and of converts is proverbial, so that they often become 'plus royal que le Roi meme,') has given us so choice an expression of its opinion on this point, and so veracious a passage of history, that I give them both for the amusement, improvement, and edification of my readers.

A DEFENSE OF FREEMASONRY

For them I crave the special attention of all Freemasons. "Furthermore, the Masonic principles of equality, of liberty, and of universality, tend to destroy civil authority, the obedience of subjects and patriotism. In France, during the last century, Voltaire, D'Alembert, and Diderot notoriously used the lodges of Masonry for preaching and proclaiming their humanitarian dogmas of Liberty, Fraternity, and Equality- with what result we need not stay to point out. As the French revolution followed quickly upon the Masonic Congress, held in France A.D. 1785, so the numerous well-planned continental revolutions of 1848, followed within twelve months upon the Strasburg Congress of Masons in 1847. We might say more in detail, but this suffices. Let our readers work out the problem and its results."

And not only are these charges most serious and alarming in themselves, but let us attend to what follows, which is still more dreadful, and, no doubt, equally founded on fact.

"In Italy and Belgium it is notorious that abandoned women have been sent by the Freemasons to early mass, to commit an awful sacrilegious theft, so that (he more political and darker Masonic sects may penetrate at their dark orgies the most diabolical blasphemies- blasphemies which could only come direct from the lodge whose Grand Master is Satan."

What fearful orgies, and under what truly demoniacal influence we Freemasons are guilty of and live habitually! How deeply do we deserve for our wicked proceedings, both in private and in public, the obloquy and aversion of our fellow men!

But as the old French saying runs, "Qui prouve trop, prouve rien," and these charges are so manifestly ridiculous and mendacious, that I can hardly believe the writer who penned them to be thoroughly sane. They say everybody is mad about something in the world, and probably this truthful and modest writer is insane on the subject of Freemasonry.

A DEFENSE OF FREEMASONRY

In England the charge is so palpably absurd, that, even the Roman Catholics affect to leave out English Freemasonry from the accusation of secret political objects and ulterior revolutionary principles. With ere the Prince of Wales, our royal brother, at our head, and with two of his august brothers at present members of our order; with so many of the noblest of the land rulers of the Craft, with so many thousands of loyal, intelligent, and educated brethren, composing our "staple" of membership, it does seem too ridiculous to have such an allegation made against our Freemasonry in Great Britain. As a fact incontestable in itself, Freemasons in the United Kingdom have always been a peculiarly loyal body, and I venture to affirm that amid the countless faithful subjects of our Queen, she has no more devoted portion of them than are to be found among the members of our Masonic Brotherhood.

The writer in the "Church Herald," though he does not dare to accuse English Freemasonry of disloyalty, makes the following outrageous and Jesuitical statement, equally veracious with his previous one, as if, though perhaps we are not a political body, a secret agglomeration and combination, we, at any rate, are an irreligious, a most irreligious combination, and so he asks this most extraordinary, and, to us, indecent question: "Finally, do our readers forget that when Wilkes was initiated into the Masonic 'Hell-fire Club' he pretended to give Communion to an ape!"

Not having ventured to repeat the popular falsehood as regards English Freemasonry being political, he imperatively declares it to be irreligious and profane, and observe, by associating it most mendaciously, with the orgies of some dissolute persons, none of whom we believe were ever Freemasons at all If they were, which we very much doubt, they did not profess any Masonic character, and were, if they were anything, a bacchanalian prototype (foolish and wicked enough in all conscience,) of that Hibernian and hilarious symposium portrayed by Lever in one of his novels, and termed the "monks of the screw."

But with such gatherings Freemasonry has not and never had the slightest connection, nor is there the most remote pretense to say so. No one with the slightest claim to the education and feelings of a gentleman could have ventured to concoct such an "olla podrida" of historical ignorance, and exploded falsehood, and cruel slander, and I feel that the writer in truth is hardly worth notice.

Were it likely to be attended with any good result, I might be induced to ask this writer- in the words of our old teacher Calcott- "Had our institution contained nothing commendable or valuable in it, it is impossible it should have existed, and been patronized by the wise, the good and great, in all ages of the world. For we cannot suppose that men, distinguished by every accomplishment that can adorn human nature, would embrace or continue in principles which they found to be nugatory, erroneous, or contemptible. Therefore the advice which Gamaliel wisely gave to the persecutors of the apostles, might with great propriety be recommended to these railers against Freemasons. They may assure themselves, that if there was no more in our institution than their little minds suggest, it would have fallen to the ground ages past; but the contrary being the case, they may safely conclude, it will continue to exist, notwithstanding any opposition, for ages yet to come."

I might also well call his attention to the indignant words of the same able writer, in the same treatise, his able answer to the "Slanderers of Masonry."

"If therefore these accusers have any remains of modesty, if the assertors of such calumny can ever blush, they are now put to the trial; for whilst they deal thus freely with the principles and proceedings of persons of the greatest honor and distinction, they are only discovering to the judicious part of mankind, the weakness of their heads and the wickedness of their hearts. How truly do they come under the standard of that description which Justus Lipsius, an eminent writer, has given us of this abominable sect, 'Calumny,' says he, 'is a filthy and pernicious infection of the tongue; generally aimed by the most wicked and abandoned part of mankind against the most worthy and deserving of esteem, and wounds them unexpectedly. And to whom is it pleasing? To the most vile, the perfidious, the talkative. But what is its source? From what origin does it proceed? From falsehood as its father, from envy as its mother, and from curiosity as its nurse.'"

But as he concludes with the following deliberate mendacious assertion, I leave him to the contempt of all veracious minds and all honest men. "We by no means assert that all Masons are like those of Italy, Belgium, and Medmenham Abbey. But the principle of Masonry being inherently and essentially anti-Christian, its darker developments follow as a matter of course, when men are ripe for them."

Abroad the charge has been made, and still is made, as we often see and now specially note, continuously and unceasingly.

If, however, there be no more truth in it generally, than in the allegations of the ritualistic writer just quoted, and in some of the heated diatribes of Roman Catholic authorities, for from them the charge mainly arises, I should not attach much store by it. Archbishop Manning has accused the German Freemasons of being revolutionary and political, which they certainly are not, and therefore such incriminations by Roman Catholic ecclesiastical authorities of Freemasons every where just now, are to some extent admittedly and certainly exaggerated. It is possible that in Germany, as elsewhere, owing to an internecine war always going on in some countries abroad, most unwisely in my opinion, between religionists and Freemasons, (though we in England know nothing of such a state of things, since we treat all such attacks with silent contempt), there may have been some indiscreet utterances here and there. Some enthusiastic brethren in Germany and elsewhere may have been somewhat loud in their protestations against Ultramontane attacks and Jesuit inculpations, but, as a rule, German Freemasonry especially, is not political, or mixed up with any socialistic or destructive theories in any degree.

But it is, I fear, inevitable, that in the discussions which will arise about Freemasonry, and in its promulgation of its universal principles, in its aspirations for light and knowledge and free discussion, and full toleration, and liberty of thought, and comprehensiveness of teaching, the Masonic writers in those foreign countries must come into collision with the Church of Borne, little approving of private judgment, and not much more anxious to encourage intellectual culture or mental development.

If it be true that in Germany or elsewhere, there are on both sides heated partisans and unfair controversialists, a fact which all "logomachies" in the world have only too sadly made evident, if nevertheless, it be admitted that some brethren hold extreme views, I cannot allow that the German Freemasons can in any way fairly be termed a political, or a revolutionary, or a socialistic organization. It is a cruel calumny on an honorable and cultivated, and loyal body of men. And we should not lose sight of one fact among these deplorable and discreditable assaults on our usually peaceful and most orderly order, that the Church of Rome in this, as in some other matters, is a little behind the present state of things, and the actual facts of the case.

The Roman curia and the Roman Catholic authorities generally, are taking all these facts from "excerpta" of the old Jesuit slanders, and the all but forgotten impeachments of Freemasonry in the last century, from the idle suspicions of ignorant and adverse critics, from shameless self-accusing perjurers, and from sensational "Explanations" and "Revelations."

Freemasonry proper has nothing to do with socialism or

revolution, with atheists or "illumines." It cares little for an "universal philosophy," and still less for the mystical explanations of a diluted Pantheism. It has no concern with any of those humanitarian schools of thought and practice, which in the last as the present age have established and developed themselves, still less does it take any cognizance of Communistic action, or Socialistic aspirations. Indeed, the true principles of Freemasonry are entirely opposed to such pernicious teaching in civil life, as well in psychological inquiries or in religious controversy.

Fremasonry, on the contrary, ever inculcates love of country, the maintenance of order, the rights and the duties of property, family affection, the sanctity of home, the importance of religion, loyalty to the supreme authority, obedience to the laws of the land, and goodwill to all men. But while I say this, I feel bound as an honest man, looking from my English Masonic point of view, to condemn some of those foolish and ill-timed manifestos which some foreign grand lodges seem to like to issue, and which tend only, in my humble opinion, to alienate religious people still more, to antagonize the Romish Church unnecessarily and immeasurably, and to engender doubt and disseminate suspicions in respect of the real object and true teaching of Freemasonry.

Nothing is so much to be regretted, I venture to repeat my opinion, as when we hear and see a grand lodge or body of Freemasons wasting its strength, weakening its position, and throwing away its means and its time, by ceaseless and violent attacks on the "Pope," and the "Ultramontanes," or the "negri," or the "Jesuits," or on religious bodies of any kind.

It is not, and never was intended to be, the true work of Freemasonry. It cannot be considered either its mission or its rightful occupation. In France and in Belgium, English Masons are sometimes shocked by the open exclusion of the Bible from the Lodges, and by the public discussions of many unfitting matters, more or less political, and of such subjects above all, as "La morale sans Dieu." Anything more hurtful to Freemasonry, or more unmasonic, cannot well be conceived. Facts like these unfortunately tend to give color to the complaints of Home.

Wherever such a state of things exists it always invariably demonstrates this, that the practical efforts and higher labors of Freemasonry are few and far between, and that the best manifestation of its own Batted principles is sadly dwarfed and impeded by this din of controversy, and this cruel overflow of unprofitable strife. There is a time, no doubt, "to speak and a time to be silent," there is a period when defense is needful and avowal of our honest teaching is not only permissible, but imperatively required.

But, making every allowance, therefore, for involuntary controversy or relentless antagonism, I still feel how much better it would be for many of our continental brethren, if they would but remember how Freemasonry is ever most truly evidenced by its works of charity and benevolence, better far than by quasi-skeptical orations, and partisan declamations, and the heated strife of words and of opinion. I am quite aware that the position of some of our foreign brethren is both difficult and peculiar in this respect. For the Church of Borne, in her relentless spirit, regards alike with intolerant suspicion and condemnation, and places under one irrational interdict, Freemasonry everywhere just now, and I also feel that often it is almost too much for human nature not to resist and not to retaliate.

But I yet think that the more dignified position of Freemasonry undoubtedly is to pass by all such calumniators in silence, to live down such calumnies calmly and carefully, and to devote itself uncomplainingly to its high and holy duties, the practical carrying out of true benevolence, kindly sympathy, and open-hearted charity, alike for those of the craft who need our aid, as for mankind itself at large.

A DEFENSE OF FREEMASONRY

Here is our best answer alike to ecclesiastical censures and unceasing opposition, to the accusation of malevolence, and the bitterness of unkindly treatment.

Freemasonry and Freemasons cannot be wrong or do wrong here, and I would therefore urge on all my younger brethren especially in foreign countries, who may chance to read this defense of our common order, to separate themselves at once from any political agitation or religious controversy, and to divest themselves of any semblance even of participation in questions which are in truth external to Freemasonry.

Whatever the acts or accusations of their antagonists may be, whatever edicts or anathemas they may have to meet, they will receive the sympathy and support of all true Freemasons, the more so because in all honesty of purpose, and fidelity to Masonic principles, they seek to develop in actual labors of love and exertions of philanthropic and fraternal devotion, without excitement and without complaint, the great distinguishing principles of universal Freemasonry.

IV. I have now to deal with a fourth practical objection to Freemasonry, which, to say the truth, though apparently very serious, is not at all so in reality- at least, to my mind. It is this, that Freemasonry imposes and entails upon its members the taking of "unlawful oaths."

What are unlawful oaths is a question we must answer in the first place clearly and fully, and, having done so, we can then go on to deal with the objection. There can be, I think, but one reply to such a query. Those oaths are clearly unlawful, I think that all will agree, which are forbidden to be imposed or to be taken by the Legislature of this or any other country.

All oaths are clearly not unlawful, such as those which are constantly- nay, hourly, called for and administered in courts of justice, or which are ordered or sanctioned by ancient usages or special enactment.

The "onus probandi" therefore clearly falls upon our opponents to make plain that any alleged Masonic obligation or oaths are forbidden by the Legislature.

But, as the existence of Freemasonry as a secret society is openly recognized and protected by the laws of our land, as regards Freemasonry in Great Britain, at any rate, the objection is clearly altogether unsound and untenable.

Nothing can be unlawful which the law permits.

I have already previously said that, if anywhere Freemasonry is forbidden in its secret character by the laws of the State, to exist as secret, or to enforce any binding obligations equally in secret, there, in my opinion, no Freemason has a right, and no true brother would seek, to run counter to the laws of that country which may for a time become the place of his residence, or afford him its protection.

But Mr. Kerr, a recent assailant of Freemasonry, a Scotch Reformed Presbyterian minister of Greenock, takes another ground, that our Masonic system in this respect does dishonor to the "Ordinance of the oath" in Reformed Presbyterian terminology, and takes God's name in vain, being alike rash and profane swearing. Now, first of all, whatever force Mr. Kerr's objections may have for the members of his own community, they have none for others, or for Freemasons, inasmuch as Freemasons themselves are as good judges as Mr. Kerr, or the Reformed Presbyterian Synods of Glasgow and Edinburgh, of what may be fairly called "rash and profane swearing."

Therefore, as far as Freemasons are concerned, Mr. Kerr's objections under this head, are clearly "nihil ad rem," and they will pass them by altogether, for this reason among others, that they themselves, as Freemasons, alone are the best judges of the need, or importance, or rightful requirement of any obligation.

But I would also beg to observe here, and remind my brethren, that Mr. Kerr illustrates his views, and bases his allegations or quotations mainly from a person who boasts that he is a deserter from the Banners of Freemasonry, and, certainly, no deserter, on his own confession, ever better deserved to be marked with the letter D. As such- his evidence is tainted aborigine, and his witness very questionable. And I decline, therefore, as my brethren, would decline, to enter into any argument founded on evidence of such a class, as it bears openly before all men the stigma and confession of deliberate treachery and perjury on its very face. Good Mr. Kerr, with Jesuitical casuistry, lays down this most baneful maxim, that Freemasons are not bound to keep the oaths he says are imposed on them, because they may be and are, in their opinion and in his, or in that of the Reformed Presbyterian Synods, opposed to the law of God.

I sadly wonder to see the good man in such bad company, and with such Romanizing tendencies, for though it is not the first time in history that Calvinism like Jesuitism has taken up those injurious propositions, "The end justifies the means," "You may do evil that good may come," and that there is a "dispensing power" vested in an ecclesiastical body, by which it can even relax the binding nature of an obligation; I confess that I did not expect to hear such a recommendation from a Reformed Presbyterian minister, and to be told that it is sanctioned by two Reformed Presbyterian Synods. It is really most alarming.

I think, that I need only add on this subject, that it is one with which, in reality, the Church nor any religious body has anything to do, and that it can only be decided and adjudicated on by Freemasons themselves.

A DEFENSE OF FREEMASONRY

For I cannot conceive that there is more objection "a priori" to a Masonic obligation, be it what it may, than there is to the oath still taken by many of the city guilds, or any of the oaths of administration imposed by long usage, or by public or private acts of Parliament.

And therefore, though a good many weak minded persons make a great deal of this very objection, we, as Freemasons, need not care to say more about it, as it is a matter alone for our own government, arrangements, and judgment, which no other authority has anything to do with whatever. Of all assailants the Church of Rome, in its objections, is most inconceivably rash and indefensible.

It has secret societies, and secret vows, and secret oaths in plenty, and certainly for the Roman Catholics, or any other religious body under this head, to object to a similar system because not approved of by each particular community, is a relic of ecclesiastical interference and tyranny, which the sooner each of them surrenders the better.

V. There is one more objection I have to notice, and that is- that Freemasonry encourages habits of excessive conviviality. There was a time when in accordance with the fashion of the hour, even Freemasonry shared the universal customs of society and of the age.

But that state of things, like a good many other habits and manners of the times, has gradually past away, and for some years, our Masonic meetings have for the most part, been marked by much reticence of social indulgence, and commendable abbreviation of the hours of refreshment.

We should never forget, I venture to think, however, that Freemasonry is a social institution, and that its very sociality has a great and abiding charm for many a hard-worked man of business, for many a toiling professional, for many a laborious litterateur.

Many of my readers will recall today pleasant hours of fraternal converse and social intercourse in the "days that are no more" and, as wise and tolerant persons as Freemasons, we should always, it seems to me, make due allowance for the social point-of-view of the question. Indeed, I venture also to think, and to say, that he must have a churlish disposition or a contracted mind who can find fault with innocent conviviality, or the agreeable hours of free-hearted intimacy and cheerful good-fellowship.

In our great zeal for Freemasonry, while we always sternly discourage and suppress all tendencies to riot or excess, or late hours, or merely convivial assemblies, we should avoid, I cannot but express my humble opinion, laying down too strict a rule, or too ascetic regulations for our Masonic social gatherings.

And just as we should not too much devote ourselves to the "knife and fork degree," to late "sederunts," and "early hours," after the chimes of midnight have long since sounded for many a Masonic brother "Shallow" as of yore, so we should not seek to drive away the sociality of Freemasonry, or to lay down injunctions of unforcible strictness, or deprive many worthy men and good Masons of some cheerful relaxation, and of necessary adjournments from "labor" to "refreshment."

Freemasonry has long since outgrown and lived down the calumny, that it is a purely convivial meeting, a club of good fellows; and therefore we should always seek, in this as in all other matters, to find the golden mean of moderation and propriety between excess and defect, and then the charge so often made against our order that it fosters late hours and bad habits, would soon entirely pass away and be forgotten. If ever such an accusation could fairly be made against Freemasonry, it was at a time when all societies and meetings, and even private life itself, were marked by the same one law of exaggerated hospitality, but that tendency has long since yielded to other and better and higher views on the subject.

At no time, I make bold to say, could such an allegation be made against our order with fewer claims for truth, and less cause for real complaint than at the present time. I have now gone through all these many heads of objection, because I felt it incumbent on me to do so; but, I confess, that when I have come to the last of them, I feel greatly relieved that my labor has ended. For I realize more than ever how weak, how pitiful, how idle, how worthless they all are.

Freemasonry resembles, in my mind, a great and goodly building, which, surrounded by fog and enveloped in haze, looks in the distance a shapeless form to the human eye when shrouded in the all embracing atmosphere of mist and cloud. But as the sun pours down its glorious light, and the fog bank "lifts" and slowly fades away, this same building is disclosed in all its stateliness of architecture and beauty of contour to the enraptured visitor and spectator.

And so is it with our good old order, and the great institution of Freemasonry, for great it assuredly is, and great I trust it long will continue to be, despite the cavils of some, the injustice of others, and the opposition and even malediction of the zealot or of the intolerant.

As all these idle accusations melt into nothingness and seem utterly to disappear like drifting clouds, as all these perverse clamors are stilled, as the heated incrimination is dismissed, as the unrighteous anathema is forgotten and forgiven, Freemasonry seems to stand out clearer and more majestic than ever to our mental apprehension and our fraternal sight!

It appeals even more forcibly than ever alike to our intellect and our sympathies, to our loyalty, and to our affections.

For, after all, what have these attacks and assailants served to show? Is it not simply this? That though Freemasonry may be misunderstood by the ignorant, depreciated by the credulous, and condemned by the intolerant, it still is able to pursue its course happily undeterred and undaunted, and to claim the active obedience and to deserve the faithful allegiance of countless members who dignify the order by their high character, their spotless integrity, their exalted worth, their true morality, and their many admirable qualities of heart and mind.

Freemasonry has, like all human institutions, its seasons of vigor and languor, of earnestness and apathy, of success and of failure, of increase and of decrease; yet never was there a time in our annals when, on every side of us, we behold symptoms of a most prosperous order and of a rapidly expanding organization.

Why is this? But simply because, of late years especially, Freemasonry, true to itself and to its own tenets, has anxiously endeavored to give a practical turn, so to say, to all its universal principles and all its esoteric teaching, by making its pretensions square with its profession, and by manifesting to all men by many an undoubted proof that its labors of charity, and benevolence, and sympathy, and relief are coextensive with its ancient system of declamation and oration, of avowal and of comprehension. And therefore it is that Freemasonry may indeed boldly reply to any impugner or skeptic of its reality and its benefits. If you want to know what Freemasonry is, if you are desirous of ascertaining what Freemasonry seeks to be and to do, "Si quaeris, circumspice."

Remember what are our yearly exertions in the cause of true charity; observe how we seek to assist infirmity, to comfort old age, to educate the orphans, and to give relief and to extend a helping hand to many a poor, distressed brother, or his widow and her children, in the trying hour of earthly calamity, or in the presence of bereavement, or in the sad season of earthly misfortune or decay. Now it has been said, though very unjustly, that Freemasonry is both egotistical and selfish in its professed charitable exertions.

But, as has been well remarked by an able American writer already quoted, "The principle that governs Freemasonry in all its branches in the distribution of its charities and the exercise of all the friendly affections is that which was laid down by St. Paul for the government of the infant church at Galatia: 'As we have opportunity, therefore let us do good unto all men, especially unto those who are of the household of faith.' This sentiment of preference for one's own family of faith, thus sanctioned by apostolic authority, is after all but the dictate of human nature, and the words of Scripture find their echo in every heart. Blood is thicker than water, and those who have established the claim of worshiping at our altar have established the first claim on Masonic charity."

We begin with our own brethren, but we do not forget others, and, from some experience of the Masonic order, I will say this, that there are few of our fellow citizens who more earnestly seek to "do good unto all men" than the many warm-hearted members of our often undervalued but true-hearted fraternity.

When, therefore, I look at our noble charities today, and recall how large a sum we give habitually through the various channels of our great system in freewill offerings of benevolence and aid to the afflicted and deserving of our brotherhood of Freemasonry, could I find nothing more than this, I might rest my defense of Freemasonry, I feel, safely here.

But when to this I add the friendships it forms and the toleration it enjoins, when I reflect that now, as ever, it represents light as opposed to darkness, and freedom as opposed to vassalage, when I realize how it would seek everywhere to promote and inculcate intellectual culture and consistent morality, peace, and order, good will and law, reverence for God and love for man, I ask myself, what is the meaning of this paradox, that this needful and important and beneficent society is to be opposed and arraigned, calumniated and condemned!

What is this perversity of the human intelligence or of ecclesiastical teaching, which would seek to represent Freemasonry, ever a friend to humanity and concord, and religion and virtue, as the "craft of the Evil One," and its associates as members of that "Grand Lodge whose Grand Master is Satan?"

Now I do not seek to deny or to conceal from any who read this "defense" of mine that Freemasonry is not perfect, but, like all other human institutions, has its inevitable weaknesses and deficiencies. Some one has said- and I fear with some little truth, for instance- that no persons can write such unbrotherly letters as Freemasons, despite all their professions of brotherly love.

Well, if it be so, as, perhaps I must allow it may be so, Freemasons only show in this, as in everything now, that imperfection and unreality often enter into and abound in all of earthly arrangement and endeavor.

It is an old story, the difference between theory and practice, between profession and living, between words and deeds, and as long as this world lasts, we shall always have to contend with unavoidable manifestations of good and evil, of strength and weakness, of right theories but bad practice in the struggles of society and in the lives of men. But let our adversaries and accusers discover and display all the blots they like; after all, how few there are of any note and importance.

Freemasons are only men, and do not claim to be exempt either from the feelings or weakness of their brethren in the world.

All they can say and do say is, Can you find another

society, which universal and yet religious as it is and professes to be, has done so much good and so little harm among mankind? Even today, amid the outcry of heated opponents, amid the angry vehemence of ruthless intolerance, it seems to lift itself up above these seething waves of controversy, and leaving recrimination and indignation on one side, only to proclaim more carefully and anxiously than ever, its own simple and conciliatory message of peace and fraternal union to the severed and the suffering of the human race.

At the present moment, as I have just said, one of the most unrelenting adversaries of Freemasonry, whilst it has been condemning our harmless Brotherhood with the bitterest expressions of disapproval and anathema, has also raised a jubilant shout of triumph on account of the secession of Lord Ripon to that Church, and his resignation of the Grand Mastership of English Freemasonry!

But the Church of Borne has been a little premature in her exultation. Deeply as all English Freemasons regret that step for Lord Ripon's own sake, as well as for the Craft, they can only regard it and remember it in respectful silence. Able ruler, as Lord Ripon was undoubtedly, his resignation will not have the slightest appreciable effect on English Freemasonry. On the contrary, it may even tend to give a further stimulus to our rapidly augmenting lodge rolls.

Freemasons are always loyal, and the Presidency of our Royal Brother, the Prince of Wales, will be a matter of universal rejoicing to the Craft. For it will recall not only auspicious days of old, and continue that intimate and happy connection which has existed for nearly 150 years between the Royal Family and Freemasonry in this country, but it will be the best answer possible to Lord Ripon's unhappy departure from among us, and his resignation oi the highest office of Masonic dignity. For though our Order has lost, I fully admit, an accomplished chief in Lord

Ripon, it is exactly where it was before he left us, and it is not the least influenced either by his secession, or by the tone the Roman Catholic Press has thought fit to assume as regards Freemasonry.

Neither, in truth, has Freemasonry any fears as to the practical results, if the conflict be still unwisely carried on and persisted in. The Roman Catholic Church is apparently bent on the Quixotic crusade of attempting to "stamp out" Freemasonry everywhere, as well in Italy, and Belgium and Germany, as in the United States and Great Britain. Idle effort! Chimerical idea! Freemasonry today is not to be silenced or appalled by edicts or allocutions, or crushed by anathemas and excommunications. Freemasonry means to hold its own, and is holding its own manfully, even now, despite all attacks and all assailants everywhere.

And as long as it continues to do so in moderation and calmness, with logical arguments, on the true principles of Ancient, Free, and Accepted Freemasonry, so long humanly speaking, is its success certain. The only possible danger is, lest in the ardor of the contest, and the excitement of passing polemics, as Free- masons we should ever pass our proper limits, and seek to defend ourselves by language and proceedings which are at variance altogether with the great and unchanging principles and professions of our order.

Thus far the attack on Freemasonry has utterly failed, because made in defiance of the known facts of history, and the true position of affairs; because ignoring deliberately our veritable teaching, and because, above all, adducing fictitious "excerpta" from self-condemnatory slanderers, it has based its censure of us on considerations and feelings most repulsive to the moral honesty and right judgment of mankind. Nothing is so melancholy to the reflective and the reasoning, as to see how a great religious body like the Church of Rome, (to say nothing here of her petty imitators), has, in the virulence of her animosity, and the unreasonableness of her intolerance, utterly forgotten the great axioms of justice, fair-play, liberty of conscience, and truth.

She has condemned Freemasonry anew, as of old, unheard, and without giving the slightest weight to the peaceful principles, and the kindly deeds of its members, and she has done all this professedly in the name of religion and of the faith, utterly regardless of the fact, that nothing is so prejudicial in its reflex action on a Church, as the promulgation either of doctrines and declarations, which are opposed "ipso facto," to the common sense, and the right reason of mankind. Great in her inconsistency, as in her pretensions to infallibility, though abounding in secret societies herself, she has reprobated Freemasonry loudly and vehemently, mainly, apparently, because it is secret order, and because, above all, it repudiates the authority and allocutions of the Roman Pontiff.

But students of history may be induced, I think by such acts, to recall to mind that the Church of Home is indeed "semper eadem" in her opposition to all liberty of thought, and development of the intellect, and all drawing out of the conscious judgment of the enlightened moral will, and educated private personal responsibility of man. And it is greatly to be feared that, this fresh outbreak of Roman intolerance and injustice today, against our loyal and friendly brotherhood, is but another sad proof, if proof be needed, how the Roman Catholic Church of our own time, like that "whited sepulcher" of which we have been told, though outwardly abounding in professions of favor for art and science, for progress and philanthropy, for all that can adorn society, or elevate mankind, is after all, inwardly as implacable as ever. For unchanged and unrelenting she is assuredly in her deadly hostility to any profession of faith, or labor of love, which has not received the "Imprimatur" of the Romish infallibility, or is not in accordance with the traditions of that Church, which demands surrender of all that best dignifies and ennobles man's nature here, as the test of membership, and the proof of obedience.

A DEFENSE OF FREEMASONRY

It is indeed, as I said at the outset, a most remarkable fact in the history of our race, to note the tendency to persecute, and calumniate others, so prevalent among men, and even Christians; and in nothing does the Church of Rome so stand out in the annals of time, as a beacon, both of warning and of awe, as in her ceaseless efforts to emasculate the human conscience, and to do injury to the real, great, loving message of true religion.

Now I have said all this, not from any love of controversy, not from any wish to attack the Church of Rome, not from any sympathy whatever, with the heated declamations of the hour, and above all, in no spirit of disrespect or unkindness, either to the benevolent head of the Roman Catholic Church, or to Roman Catholics themselves. But I wish to put the matter clearly and fully before my brethren, as from the Church of Borne the main attacks, and the actual condemnation of Freemasonry proceed even now.

Believing, as I do conscientiously, both that the Church of Rome has nothing to do with Freemasonry, and has no right to condemn Freemasonry or Freemasons, I feel bound to enter my humble protest against the unwise and unchristian course her rulers are adopting today.

I do not for one moment dispute the right of the Church of Rome, or any religious body to make what terms of membership they respectively think right, and even to exclude Freemasons from the roll of Church members, much as I should regret that any religious body should take so foolish and so unrighteous a step.

But the Church of Rome not only does this, but professes to pass condemnation on a society which enrolls in its ranks one hundred non- Roman Catholics for one Roman Catholic. Indeed, I believe the proportion is greater. So true is Rome to her old principles of thought and action that even today, despite the evident folly of such a claim, she demands for the occupant of the "seat of St. Peter" a spiritual supervision over all Christians, and, in fact, over the whole world, and therefore professes to issue these unjustifiable edicts, in the interests of the faith, and for the promotion of virtue, charity, and truth. Now I have myself no fear of the actual result of this conflict between Freemasonry and the Roman Church, if it is to be waged by that Church, (for Freemasonry wages no war with any religious body,) if only Freemasons are true to Freemasonry, if only Freemasons are true to themselves. Otherwise I should have to believe that light would be overcome by darkness, liberty by tyranny, brotherly love by uncharitableness, and toleration by intolerance!

But what has Freemasonry really to dread?

No purely human organization, that I am aware of, is susceptible of such a defense as Freemasonry really and truly is.

Here is a society- or sodality, call it which you will- alike tolerant and straightforward, bold yet peaceable, governed by ancient laws and esoteric teaching, by an occult ceremonial, and by mysterious conditions of membership, which has brought within its goodly organization men of the most conflicting and discordant views, whether in politics or religion. Is Freemasonry to be blamed for its constitution? Can it be condemned for its proceedings?

Are the practical records of the reality of its calm and consistent professions a fair subject either for censure or ridicule? Certainly not!

Freemasonry may have its defects like any other institution of earth; it may have here and there, so to say, a stone loose or decayed in its glorious superstructure, but it has outlived so far the inroads of "Time's effacing Angers," and has survived many other institutions, small and great, which have long since vanished entirely from the face of the earth.

A DEFENSE OF FREEMASONRY

As its professions and teaching are ever those of brotherly sympathy and universal beneficence, it has sought, and not unsuccessfully sought, to carry them out in practice by many a work of unhesitating good will, and by many a labor of zealous munificence. It grants month by month large sums of relief, in its tripartite arrangements, to the indigent, the suffering, and forlorn, it offers annuities to aged Freemasons of both sexes to assist them in the decline of life or the advance of decrepitude, or the reverse of fortune, it educates the orphan sons and daughters of the brotherhood with unsparing liberality and striking success.

All these various works and efforts and institutions which demand large annual subsidies from a generous fraternity are commenced, carried on, and supported with large hearted, and praiseworthy, and even princely liberality by our great English brotherhood. Indeed, perhaps there is no one point in our English system which is so creditable to our order and to Freemasonry, as all the past history, the present position, and the annual returns of our Masonic charities.

And I will also say this:

I believe in no profession of Freemasonry which does not evidence the reality of its belief and of its principles by these evident tokens of sincerity, of having "counted the cost" of Masonic membership. The best test of all true Freemasonry is, what does it do for charity? How does it manifest brotherly love and sympathy and relief?

Whenever these indicia of the true spirit of our good old craft are wanting, depend upon it there is something wrong in that section of the Masonic family. In vain you may tell me of noble orations in the name of humanity and solidarity, in vain I may have to listen to declamatory harangues about liberty, equality and fraternity; useless it is to tell me of philanthropic aspirations, of psychological studies, of illuminating rhapsodies. If charity be wanting the rest are worthless!

I do not believe in that Freemasonry, or those Freemasons, where, and among whom nothing but a sterile logomachy or glowing declamations are endured or applauded. All these things, like the truest and happiest of ceremonial observances, like "elegant banquets" and "pleasant reunions," the "feast of reason and the flow of soul," and the high and important avocations of the "Knife and Fork Degree" itself, are, I am sorry to say, to so cynical a brother as I fear some may think me to be, but as "sounding brass or a tinkling cymbal." If Freemasonry has no manifest tokens of its inward vitality and truth to offer to the outward world besides its jewels and decorations, its speeches and its refreshment, its social gatherings and its festive board, it will soon perish utterly and vanish also in turn from the face of the earth! But so long as the Divine grace of Charity shall sweeten all its toils, and consecrate all its endeavors, so long, I believe, in the good providence of God, will Freemasonry happily survive both the changes of time and the convulsions of society, to proclaim in good will and toleration, in sincerity and benevolence, its simple, remedial, and healing teaching to mankind.

And Freemasonry, in addition to its many ("overt acts" of active sympathy and relief, offers, I think, we should not forget in conclusion, in its lodges a pleasant hour of retreat from business or care, or toil or trouble, to many a hardworking and zealous member of our fraternity.

How many long friendships have been formed in our lodge rooms? How many hours of pleasant intercourse, of heart-companionship, have there been spent? How much of innocent gaiety, and of cheerful "bonhomme" have there combined to lighten some hours of anxiety, and to cheer some toiling and weary children of men? In the lodge room, all those to whom I write, like myself, can recall many and many a joyous meeting, and many, alas! many a faded hour of pleasantness and peace, when in the flow of manhood and high spirits we could greet so gladly the smile of honest friendship, or clap the warm hand of brotherly devotion.

And if to some of us, as to the writer, the echoes are hushed today of those soft strains of tender memory, and seem to float away and vanish in the distance, they can still revisit us in some casual hour, and replenish our minds with the awakened sympathies of unforgotten moments of friendship and brotherhood "ever bright and fair."

And when to all that is purely personal, to you as to me, I venture to super-add all that is truly Masonic, both in theory and practice, in profession and in reality, I feel and hope how great a claim I have established for some credit and some respect for our venerable and useful fraternity, and that my defense of our arraigned and calumniated order is not altogether made in vain.

On the contrary, I feel it myself more strongly than ever, and, I believe, my brethren will agree with me, that as Freemasons we may rejoice to recollect and to own that we are members of our ancient and honorable craft.

To use the words of a lecture by Bro. Codrington in 1770: "Thus have I given you some account of Masonry, and qualifications necessary to make a worthy member of it; by which you see it is not a ridiculous and trifling, but a very serious and important institution; an institution founded on the most exalted principles of moral and social virtue. May we ever keep in view its noble and real design, and catch the spirit of it. May it be our glory to practice the duties it prescribes. Moral architects as we are, may we build temples for every virtue; prisons and dungeons for vice, indecency and immorality. May we be disposed to every humane and friendly office, ever ready to pour oil and wine into the wounds of our distressed brethren, and gently bind them up, (it is one of the principal ends of our institution), so that when those who speak evil or lightly of us behold our conduct, and see by our means the hungry fed, the naked clothed, the sick sustained and cherished- shall see our light so usefully shine- their evil speaking may be silenced, their foolish prejudices removed, and they may be convinced that Masonry is an useful and a venerable structure, supported by the great and everlasting pillars of wisdom, strength and beauty."

Disregarding all unjust attacks, and smiling at all intolerant opponents, we shall all of us only feel more persuaded of the benefit and importance of Freemasonry; and our prayer will be that the great Architect of the universe may long continue to bless our order with all the good gifts of Masonic unity, concord, and peace; to preserve it unharmed and unchanged in the onward and troubled career of human affairs, to fill every Masonic heart among us with true charity, care, and sympathy, each for each, for all poor and distressed Freemasons in this wide world of ours, as well as for all suffering members of the human race, and that He will deign, above all, to cement our venerable order as well by the faithful profession and the upright lives of its enrolled members, with every moral and every social virtue. So mote it be!

A DEFENSE OF FREEMASONRY

APPENDIX

WHAT IS FREEMASONRY?

"A very important question is asked in our lectures; 'What is Free-masonry?' and the ordinary reply to the query is, that it is 'a peculiar system of morality veiled in allegory and illustrated by symbols,' but the subject demands a closer examination, and a more elaborate answer, for it embraces every part of that noble science which has existed as far as we know, from time immemorial, and under whose powerful influence such wonderful results have been obtained. The question, however, is often reiterated by those who are outside our order, and sometimes with no friendly motive, for like all other human institutions it has its detractors, however pure may be its objects or spotless its career. From vain curiosity they strive to penetrate the arcana of our secrets, but happily, such efforts have hitherto proved fruitless to all who do not possess the master key by which alone they can be obtained. While such inquirers should always be discouraged! and our order close tyled against them, there are, however, many others who are prompted by truly laudable motives, and a favorable opinion preconceived of our institutions, who feel a longing desire to know something of the origin, growth and progress of that gigantic tree whose branches are spread over the entire surface of the habitable globe, and from which such abundant fruits have been gathered. The first class of inquirers to which I have alluded, are, I am happy to say, very limited in numbers, but notwithstanding their insignificance, they are very energetic and vituperative in their slanders, and in the presence of kindred spirits in feelings and inclinations are ever ready to denounce our institution as a body that should not exist, and ought at once to be put down by the strong arm of the law. We, however, can well afford to laugh at their puny threats, and treat their vaunted allocutions with all the contempt they deserve, and in the few remarks I intend to offer, I shall perhaps not again refer to a class of inquirers who possess no title, and have no claim to our consideration. As regards the latter class to which I have referred, their motives cannot be too highly commended, for, unmindful of the vulgar remarks sometimes leveled at us by those who really know nothing about the secrets and objects of our order, they seek to inquire for themselves as to the great motives which appear to have such a patent influence in inducing so many of their fellow men to unite together with no other law than that which is enforced by their own free will, to extend the light of truth, and promote the welfare and happiness of their fellow creatures. To such inquirers we give a hearty welcome, and if they want to know more of us, and how we prove that in uniting together our object is to render ourselves more extensively serviceable to our fellow creatures, we may well use the expressive epitaph on Sir Christopher Wren, and tell them to look around at the noble institutions we have provided for the deserving objects committed to our care. Like the Roman Matron Cornelia we can say, 'These are our jewels- these are the bright and shining lights of Freemasonry.' It has been said that 'on the empire of England the sun never sets' an apt and forcible illustration of the extent and power of country to which we owe our birth; but great, noble, and dazzling as is the acquisition of territory, as an inseparable and inevitable result of conquest, such victories are sometimes only obtained at the cost of thousands of lives, with desolation, ruin, and widows and orphans following in their train But with regard to Freemasonry, although its domain is even far more extended- although as regards its influence the sun is always at its meridian- it brings no such pangs in her bright career, for hers is the mission of peace and good-will to all mankind. Her conquests are great, noble, and bloodless, and her mission is to extend the blessings of peace and the bounties of charity to every deserving object under heaven. Her reign commenced in the primitive period of the world, and her territory is not confined to one country, language or people, for it is spread over the entire habitable globe. It stands with a rock for its foundation, honor, truth, and virtue for its superstructure, whilst the three great pillars supporting its noble temple, are Faith, Hope, and Charity, thereby implying our faith in the Great Architect of the Universe, a hope in salvation, and to be in charity with all men. Our institution, too, can boast of its antiquity, forming the great link between the period when civilization just emerged from barbarism into an age in which it has expanded to such noble proportions. It was in the early days of Freemasonry that natural religion first beamed on man, the darkness which ushered in his existence began to disappear, his mind was insensibly drawn to the contemplation of the works of nature, and up through them to Nature's God. Step by step he was led to higher and nobler aspirations, and a due reverence of the Almighty, through whose benign influence and great mercy we live, and move, and have our being. It has been well said that the Almighty Architect of the Universe has never left Himself without a faithful witness among men, as the patriarch, saved from universal desolation, has preserved the sacred fire of religion, and transmitted it pure and untainted to his descendants. Even in the rudest period the teachings cf Freemasonry were full of veneration of the Deity, and the utmost regard for His supreme wisdom and power. The first tent or tabernacle erected by Moses in the wilderness for the proper and decent celebration of Divine worship by a singular coincidence formed the great prototype and ground plan of the magnificent temple built at Jerusalem by King Solomon, which for its extent and regal splendor was at that time considered one of the wonders of the world, but great like all the edifices reared by the hands of man which were designed to last for all time, they have all disappeared from the earth, and true to the prophecy which was pronounced when they were all rich in their regal splendor, the plowshare of time has passed over their site, and not one stone has been left on another. The glories of Solomon could not preserve this stately fabric from ruin ; and the temple that was reared with such industry, skill and care, has passed away 'like the baseless fabric of a vision, and left not a wreck behind.' But what shall we say of Freemasonry, the order which King Solomon in all his glory delighted to honor. Has that shared the fate of the temple to which we have just referred?- has it like the splendid structure of our Royal founder, crumbled to the dust. To these questions we can give an emphatic answer, and say that the great Order of Freemasonry not only still exists, but has gone on increasing in strength, adding every year to its vitality, and like the sapling oak it has grown to a noble and majestic tree, under whose spreading branches the young find shelter and the old repose. And why is all this, why is it that men hitherto strangers, should thus meet on the common ground of love to each other? It may be simply expressed in a few words, because it is founded on religion, and virtue, and its precepts teach us to extend the hand of brotherly love to all who come within the charmed circle of our order. It has been well described by a brother whose name I forget, in eloquent terms, when he said, 'Amid the institutions which in all ages have best deserved the protection of sovereigns, the esteem of philosophers, and the support of mankind' our order has stood conspicuous as eminently inculcating the knowledge of the supreme God, obedience to princes, subjugation of the passions, love towards our fellow creatures, and humanity to the distressed. Works of art may show the genius of man, and the fertility of his imagination; the perfection of the sciences may mark the extent of his enterprise and spirit, but nothing can demonstrate the goodness of his heart more than Freemasonry. Whether it be in peace or war- in the calm of sunshine, of prosperity, or the bitter gales of adversity, Freemasons welcome each other with cordiality, sacrifice themselves one for another, receive with brotherly love, cherish with relief, and greet with truth those who have no other claim than fraternity, no other tie than one bond of recognition."

-Bro. H. Thompson.

THE SECRETS OF FREEMASONRY

"Freemasonry, I admit, has its secrets. It has secrets peculiar to itself; but of what do they principally consist? They consist of signs and tokens, which serve as testimonials of character and qualifications, which are only conferred after a due course of instruction and examination These are of no small value. They speak an universal language, and act as a passport to the attention and support of the initiated in all parts of the world. They cannot be lost so long as memory retains its power. Let the possessor of them be expatriated, shipwrecked, or imprisoned; let him be stripped of everything he has got in the world, these credentials remain. They have stayed the hand of the destroyer; they have softened the asperities of the tyrant; they have mitigated the horrors of captivity; they have subdued the rancor of malevolence, and broken down the barrier of political animosity. On the field of battle; in the solitudes of the uncultivated forest, or in the busy haunts of the crowded city, they have made friends men of the most hostile feelings. The most distant regions, and the most diversified conditions rush to the aid of each other, and feel special joy and satisfaction that they have been able to afford relief to a brother Mason."

-Benjamin Franklin.

A DEFENSE OF FREEMASONRY

THE DESIGN OF FREEMASONRY

"The design of the Masonic institution is to make us wiser, better, and consequently, happier. The principal subject which Masonry, as a speculative science, has to deal with is man. It seeks to unfold in him a proper appreciation of the Deity and his works, and in all his laudable undertakings to look for applause and guidance to the author of all wisdom, the Almighty ruler of the universe. His moral sensibilities are to be developed and exercised, his intellect cultivated and refined, his evil passions subdued, and all acting together in accordance with nature's laws, impress the world with the importance and dignity of the individual man. When we take into consideration that he is made in the image and likeness of the Supreme Architect of the Universe, and that the same Almighty Being breathed into his nostrils the breath of life, we will realize in a measure the importance of the subject. In our physical construction we are fearfully and wonderfully made, presenting instances of astonishing endurance and tenacity to life, and instances to impress us how easily the 'silver cord is loosed' and the vital spark suddenly extinguished. While as Masons we contemplate and properly estimate the mysterious processes of human life, and are filled with wonder at the infinite wisdom and knowledge of a being who governs and directs the pulsations of every human heart, as well as the movements of worlds and systems of worlds which geometry reveals, and by hypothesis, worlds and systems of worlds beyond the reach of human observation and conception; yet feel grateful that he has implanted in man the noblest of all gifts, reason, which, if properly exercised and guided by the Great Light in Masonry, (the Holy Bible), which always has a prominence on the Masonic altar, 'that book of books', the only book by which the bark of man can navigate the sea of life, and gain the port of bliss securely, will direct his steps through the intricate paths of life to a safe and peaceful haven. Freemasonry is designed to take hold of man in his rude and natural state, and, by developing the nobler powers of his nature, prepare him intellectually and morally for the various duties he may be called upon to perform, 'while traveling through this vale of tears.' It recognizes the fact that unless the passions of man, that rage within his breast like an ocean amid a storm, be regulated and subdued, they will operate as a destroying element, as a consuming fire; consequently he is met at the very threshold of the Temple, and in the most impressive manner made acquainted with its absolute and vital importance. Tongues cannot depict the wretchedness, suffering and misery produced in the world by the unrestrained exercise of the passions Men may be found in every station and avenue of life with shattered constitutions, ruined fortunes, and blasted hopes, showing the results unmistakeably, in their presentation, of the fearful wreck their passions have been making in the individual man; and when we take into consideration the mental anguish and suffering occasioned by these acts to those more intimately connected with them, as well as the effect upon society in general, we cannot but realize the importance of this branch of Masonic teaching; for by teaching the individual man to control his passions you prepare him in the aggregate to be good citizens and. rulers, under whose harmonious and enlightened sway, no foreign or fratricidal war would drench a land with blood, or fill it with the weeping and wailing of orphans. The human passions is a theme which is dwelt upon in the Holy Scriptures, where we may find 'line upon line and precept upon precept.' The minister, while standing behind the sacred desk, proclaiming the everlasting Gospel of peace, struggles with all his powers of mind and soul, for the reduction of this disturbing and destroying element. Learned disquisitions on the same subject may be found among the writings of moralists and philosophers of all ages of the world. Freemasonry, from remote antiquity, from her beautiful and harmonious system and regularity, leads her subjects step by step, and, by keeping constantly before their minds the essential qualifications of a good Mason, touches and opens their hearts gradually to receive those principles of morality and virtue which prompt them to deeds of charity, 'to soothe the unhappy, to sympathize with their misfortunes, to compassionate their miseries, and to restore peace to their troubled minds.' Her moral code cannot be improved- it needs no revising, enlarging, or changing. It is founded on the immutable truths of the Bible, indisputable and eternal. Through a long succession of centuries, amid the wreck of empires and the darkness of the middle ages, she preserved her light undimmed, and emerged in all her beauty and brilliancy, like gold tried in the furnace. No other system ever devised by men to impress on mankind great moral truths has ever had the power to unite men of different nationalities, religions, habits and customs, scattered over every other part of the habitable globe, to work together in harmony, and all seeking to purify the moral atmosphere, teaching mankind .the necessity of walking uprightly in their several stations, before God and man, squaring their actions by the square of virtue, and reminding them that they are traveling on the level of time toward 'that undiscovered country from whose borne no traveler ever returns.' There is something that inspires us with thoughts above ourselves when we contemplate the genius, the pure spirit of Masonry. No special allurements have ever induced her to overstep her ancient landmarks and parade her beauties ostentatiously before an indifferent world; but the world nevertheless feels the benefit of her labors, like gentle dew falling in the stillness of the midnight hour. She encompasseth not sea and land to make proselytes, but exerts an unobtrusive influence upon the hearts of men, which prompts them to seek admission within her temple walls; she presents no allurements to those who have no higher motive than to forward selfish aims and selfish ambitions, but those who drink in her pure spirit she elevates in the scale of morality and virtue, and proves indeed a fostering mother. Happiness is what Freemasonry seeks to confer upon her votaries, and happiness is what God designed for man by endowing him with mental and moral power, and making him lord of creation, spreading out before him nature in all her profusion, and inviting him to explore her to her most concealed recesses. She invites to the study of astronomy, that he may learn to admire the starry heavens, and take in and comprehend the beauty of that faultless dome, studded with those beautiful gems of the night, compared with which all man's ingenuity and skill, even in the palmiest days of Grecian and Roman architecture, sink into insignificance. She invites to the study of mathematics, by a proper knowledge of which he may be made to feel the insignificance of all human calculations compared with the calculations of Him whose problems are beyond the possibility of human solution. His attention is called to the five senses of human nature- hearing, seeing, feeling, smelling, and tasting- that the world of wonders by which he is surrounded may contribute to his happiness, enabling him to find 'tongues in trees, books in the running brooks, and good in everything.' He looks abroad upon the varied fields of nature, and although poor, perhaps, compared with those whose mansions glitter in his sight, calls the delightful scenery all his own- 'his are the mountains, and the valleys his; and the resplendent rivers his by a peculiar right, and by an emphasis of interest his, whose eyes they fill with tears of holy joy, whose heart with love, and whose exalted mind with thoughts of that unwearied One who planned and formed, and still upholds, a world.'"

"It is our privilege by the exemplification of Masonic virtues in our family circles, to lead them to feel that the white apron is not a meaningless badge; but an emblem of all that is lovely and noble in human character; and while it is our duty to watch with a jealous eye that no innovations are suffered to creep in and destroy or mar the harmony and beauty of her proportions, yet we must not forget that we live in an age of progress unexampled in the history of the world, where the means for the improvement of the mind lie scattered around us like leaves in autumn weather; and that duty to our God, to ourselves, and the claims society has upon us, alike demand that we should not let these golden opportunities pass unheeded and unimproved. It needs no labored argument to prove that Masonry demands intellectual development at the hands of her chosen disciples. At the very outset of a Mason's career, she puts on the yoke of mental discipline, for the purpose of inducing mental culture, and makes it, to a certain extent, a pre-requisite to his standing before men and brethren as a Free and Accepted Mason; and if this is necessary at the very outset, how much more necessary to his advancement if he desires to understand the principles which have kept a society together in one unbroken mysterious chain running back for more than four thousand years- if he wishes to understand 'the secret sympathy, the silver link, the silken tie, which heart to heart and mind to mind can bind'- if he wishes to hold sympathetic communion with a 'Rob Morris,' whose soul stirring productions seem in unison and harmony with the music of the spheres, he must study as he has, breathe the spirit of our glorious institution, which entertains no narrow, contracted views of the principles which it inculcates ; but on the contrary dispersing sectionalism and bigotry like mist before the beams of the morning sun- teaching man that catholic and liberal view of duty which embraces all mankind, wherever located, as having one destiny- teaching him solemn lessons of morality, and impressing him with the truth that 'leaves have their time to fall, and flowers to wither at the north wind's breath, and stars to set; but Thou, Thou hast all seasons for Thine own, oh, death!' an institution eminently calculated to exercise in harmonious union all the capacities of the intellect and all the most exquisite powers of the soul; filling man with a high sense of his duty to God, to his neighbor, and the various relations he sustains to his family, enabling him to delight in the soul kindling flashes in the eyes of his children, indicating an ardent desire for more light, and qualifying him to nurture the budding thought, to bloom and ripen for immortality, ennobling and enriching everything with which he comes in contact; developing and enlarging the powers with which a beneficent Creator has endowed him; leveling, plumbing, and squaring him for that upper and glorious temple, where the Supreme Architect of the Universe presides."- Bro. W. B. R. Runyan N.S.

A DEFENSE OF FREEMASONRY

THE CONSTITUTION OF FREEMASONRY

"In its constitutional character, Masonry is essentially a moral institution. The uninitiated frequently ask: 'Has Masonry a creed? Is it a religious order?' Some of my brothers will give different answers to these questions- many, I know, view it from a different stand-point than the one I take, In what I may say of it I wish to be understood as speaking but my own views. Oar order has no authorized mouth- piece; no human oracle, whose voice of sentiments can bind the Craft. Nothing I might say could bind it, or compromise it, even if I had the will to do so. As I read our tenets, and interpret, the theory, practice and spirit, our order, Masonry has a creed. It is a religious order. Our Great Light is the Holy Bible! From that we take our creed. That creed is, Faith in God, Hope in Immortality, Charity to all mankind. This is our way, so plain, so simple, 'that the wayfaring man, though a fool, cannot err therein.'"

"Faith, that there is a God, a faith taught us by nature, taught us by every system of worlds, and every world of every system, taught us by material creation, above, neath us, taught us by every mountain that rears its lofty summit to the skies, by every valley, with its emerald carpet and sun-lit flowers, by every season and by every creature. A faith taught us by Revelation, by that Great Book- that light shining through all the earth, taught us by prophet, priest, and seer, taught us in the living words, in characters blazing from every page- all proving, with the certainty of the demonstration, there is a God."

Our faith is the stable chain that binds us to the Infinite;
The voice of a deep life within,
That will remain, until we crowd it thence.

Our Hope.

A DEFENSE OF FREEMASONRY

> Tis the divinity that stirs within us;
> Tis Heaven itself that points out a hereafter,
> And intimates eternity to man.

"Not only does Masonry point us the way, and bid us hope, but urges, commands, begs us to follow it:"

> Eternal Hope! when yonder spheres sublime
> Pealed their first notes to sound the march of time,
> Thy joyous youth began, but not to fade,
> When all the sister planets have decay'd!
> When rapt in fire, the realms of ether glow,
> And Heav'ns last thunder shakes the earth below,
> Thou, undismayed shall o'er the ruins smile,
> And light thy torch at nature's funeral pile.

"The Great Apostle says, 'Now abideth faith, hope and charity, but the greatest of these is charity.' As Masons understand it, this charity refers to all men, but more particularly to our brother Masons, 'wheresoever dispersed throughout the habitable globe.' Nor is that charity alone which contributes to the pecuniary necessities of our brothers, but that God-like charity which, like a mantle, covers their errors, puts the most lenient and favorable construction on all their acts. Gathering to our hearts rays from the Great Light ever present in our lodge, we are taught to be charitable to the opinions, to the actions, to the motives of men, patient with their errors, forgiving when they retract. Beautifully has the poet described our Masonic charity;"

> Pure is her aim, and in her temper mild,
> Her wisdom seems the weakness of a child;
> She makes excuses when she might condemn,
> Reviled by those who hate her, prays for them!
> Suspicion lurks not in her heartless breast;

The worst suggested she believes the best:
Not soon provok'd, however stung and teas'd,
And if perhaps made angry, soon appeased;
She rather waives than will dispute her right
And injured, makes forgiveness her delight.

"Such a creed needs neither priest or prelate to interpret; no learned criticism to explain; no profound erudition, hunting up far-fetched meanings for his words. The way to it does not lie through the dark, turbulent and disturbed streams of religious controversy. The words mean just what they say- they are short; scarcely as many letters as other creeds have volumes. Is not this a religion? If you define religion to be the close, technical following of some particular theory or dogma, cut out and grooved, and fitted together by human hands, it is Not religion. If it consists in a mind and heart imbued with a love for God and for man, is it not religion? We are charged with being an unchristian organization. The Divine Teacher, while on earth, said, 'Thou shalt love the Lord thy God with all thy heart, and with all thy mind, and with all thy strength- this is the first and great commandment; and the second is like unto it, thou shalt love thy neighbor as thyself. On these two commandments hang all the law and the prophets. That is the Christian creed! That has been the Masonic creed from the earliest institution of our order."

"'Thou shalt love the Lord thy God.' Masonry enjoins it. To Him her temples are erected. Without that, without an abiding love, trust, and belief in him, the bright temple of Masonry, with all its glittering jewels and dazzling ornaments, must be for ever shut within impenetrable walls. He who has not this must pause at her outer door- his footsteps can never resound in her halls. 'Thou shalt love thy neighbor as thyself.' He who neglects this is no Mason. Cover him with the gorgeous paraphernalia of our order, place him on the topmost pinnacle of our column, if his heart is not filled with this, if, in his outward walk, by thought, by word, by action, he fails to show forth this, he is no Mason. In vain would the door of every lodge and temple throughout the world fly open at his knock; in vain would all our learning, and tradition, and mysteries flow from his tongue glibly as oil, if, in his heart of hearts, he is not thoroughly imbued with this principle; if he lacks in this, he hath not part or lot with us. This, ladies and gentlemen, as I understand it, is the religion of Freemasonry. Holding such a broad creed, is it any wonder that upon it, so many men of such varied feelings and principles, races and nationalities, can and do gather. We are not a church, in the ordinary acceptation of that term. Masonry bows to no idols, worships no graven images, deifies no mortals; the consciences of her votaries lay themselves bare to no human eye; no human mediator stands between them and their God. Resting upon the Word of God as . the source of all light, they look upon their faith as well founded. Taught by it that there is an immortality beyond the grave, and guided by its teachings, with love for all, and charity towards every man, they hope to reach the Celestial Lodge on High. Is it any sacrifice of faith, any lowering of the true Christian character so to think?"

"Paul, the great expounder, traveling to Athens, found an altar, with the inscription, 'to the Unknown God.' At that altar had probably knelt Plato, Socrates, and all the great minds who illuminated Grecian art, philosophy and literature. From it had ascended incense, offered by Jews and Greeks, by the Latin and Barbarian. The stones around it had been pressed by the knees of strangers from every land, and searchers after the Unknown God from every clime. And now knelt there the great Apostle and expounder of the new religion. As his feet pressed the steps of that altar, and as his voice went forth to that vast throng, think you that no thought of the others who had worshiped there crossed his mind? Do you imagine that he thereby lost his Christian character, that he was lowered in his Christian faith? Did it not rather elevate his thoughts; did it not lessen his feeling of isolation, that thought, that back of him stood an altar around which all heathendom might kneel? That at that altar had probably been offered prayers and sacrifices by the greatest and best and purest in the earth! Did it not add power to his voice, new light to his words with his hearers, that he, a stranger preaching a new-fangled doctrine, could yet kneel at their altar, and reach his God from it? Such an altar Masonry erects; not inscribed to an Unknown God, but to the God of Abraham, of Isaac and Jacob- an altar at which all who recognize His existence, and strive to do His works, may kneel, and together lift their voices to his throne of Grace. Masonry represents no particular sect or denomination. We unite in our brotherhood men who agree upon the great doctrines and fundamental principles that underlie morality, godliness, charity. We say to our initiates, believe in these, beyond that we do not go; on all other and non-essential matters, follow the dictates of your own reason, obey your own conscience. It matters not to us whether one brother believes in the fallibility of the Pope, and another regards him as anti-Christ; whether one clings to Christian perfection and another to total damnation; whether one holds to infant baptism and another condemns it; whether one talks of an apostolic succession and another of an universal ministry. We say to all, have faith in God, hope in immortality, practice charity to all men; this is our Alpha and Omega." -Bro. George Reynolds.

THE END